ADVANCE

"This book is a must read for any traveler who wants to experience the most enriching kind of travel—immersing yourself in a different culture and letting adventure play out at its own pace. As a woman who spent two years traveling slowly, I know what an incredible collection of tools and tips it will be for those who want to experience the next level in travel. If you're wondering how to make your travel dream a reality, you have only to start with the first chapter."

— **Michelle Lamphere,** Author of *The Butterfly Route*, Author of *Tips for Traveling Overland in Latin America*, and travel blogger at SturgisChick.com

"*Slow Travel* is a guide that takes both the heart and the brain into consideration. This book walks the reader through the powerful process of blending one's passion and dreams with concrete, practical actions to transform one's view of life and how it can be lived."

— **Katie Clancy,** Director of *Do Good as You Go* – A global volunteer network of independent travelers, DoGoodAsYouGo.org

"I am all for slow travel, and Jennifer breaks it all down for even the most nervous of travelers to comprehend. In her book, *Slow Travel,* she presents you with easy to follow steps and provides questions so you can determine your why and plan your route. She covers important issues such as budgets and unplugging from your current life—two factors that will ensure that things go as smoothly as possible. While you cannot always prepare for every eventuality on a slow travel trip, Jennifer takes out much of the guesswork so you can be as organized as you can possibly be."

— **Michelle Tupy,** Author of *An Unexpected Kindness* and travel blogger at AndOffWeWent.com

"Forty years ago, when I was just starting out on my life as a traveler, taking those first tentative steps into the far reaches of the globe, I had no idea what to expect. I just went, and figured it all out by trial and error. I can't even imagine how much easier it would have been—and how many misadventures I would have avoided—if I had had a book like *Slow Travel* to guide me, comfort me, and tell me it would all be okay.

"Fortunately, for those embarking on their adventure now, that help is right at their fingertips."

— **Nancy Sathre-Vogel,** Author of *Changing Gears: A Family Odyssey to the End of the World* and travel blogger at FamilyonBikes.org

SLOW TRAVEL

SLOW TRAVEL

Escape the

Grind and

Explore the

World

JENNIFER M. SPARKS

NEW YORK

LONDON • NASHVILLE • MELBOURNE • VANCOUVER

Slow Travel

Escape the Grind and Explore the World

© 2019 Jennifer M. Sparks

Published in New York, New York, by Morgan James Publishing in partnership with Difference Press. Morgan James is a trademark of Morgan James, LLC. www.MorganJamesPublishing.com

ISBN 978-1-64279-228-7 paperback
ISBN 978-1-64279-229-4 eBook
Library of Congress Control Number: 2018910322

Cover & Interior Design by:
Megan Whitney Dillon
Creative Ninja Designs
megan@creativeninjadesigns.com

In an effort to support local communities, raise awareness and funds, Morgan James Publishing donates a percentage of all book sales for the life of each book to Habitat for Humanity Peninsula and Greater Williamsburg.

Get involved today! Visit
www.MorganJamesBuilds.com

For Quinn. May you always believe in yourself, know that you are loved, and be able to recognize the beauty and strength in the world around you.

CONTENT

Introduction   1

Chapter One: Finding a Better Way to Travel   7

Chapter Two: What Is Slow Travel?   21

Chapter Three: Why Go?   33

Chapter Four: Is It Safe?   41

Chapter Five: Deciding Where to Go   53

Chapter Six: Affording Your Dream Trip   63

Chapter Seven: Making the Break   75

Chapter Eight: Unplugging Your Life   85

Chapter Nine: Staying Healthy   97

Chapter Ten: What to Pack   107

Chapter Eleven: Overcoming Roadblocks   119

Conclusion: My Wish for You   125

Acknowledgements   129

Thank You   133

About the Author   135

INTRODUCTION

*"The world is a book and those who do not
travel read only one page."*

St. Augustine

G inny remembers the first time she felt it. She was wandering happily through a beautiful resort campground. Large oak and maple trees provided a pleasant canopy of cool shade on an otherwise hot day. The narrow road that she walked upon was empty of cars which made for a very pleasant stroll. "Born to Run" by Bruce Springsteen played over the loud speaker and she found herself singing and dancing along as she walked.

She was 11 years old and was on a weeklong vacation with her family. While the rest of her family was still back at their campsite, Ginny had just come from the daily arts and craft activity for all the kids staying at the resort. As she strolled along the gravel road, she realized an amazing feeling for the first time in her life. She felt an enormous sense of freedom.

She was free to explore the large campground to her heart's content. Free to walk around by herself without her parents. Free to take in the wondrous natural beauty on her own terms. Free to swim in the nearby lake with the new friends that she'd met. Free to come and go from her family's camping trailer without the usual barrage of questions that she would get if they were at home. It felt amazing.

Once she had a taste of that freedom, she wanted more of it. She tried to recreate situations like that one, but she found that the feeling of freedom was elusive. Growing up meant more responsibilities that seemed to counter the carefree feeling she sought. Early responsibilities—like getting good grades in school, doing chores around the house, and taking care of her younger brother and sister—were soon replaced by studying in college and working 15 hours per week in her part-time job.

Then she was offered a wonderful opportunity. When Ginny was 19, she was invited to spend part of her summer backpacking in Europe with her good friend, Kate. Kate had grown up in the UK and had traveled before, so Ginny agreed to go along even though she had no idea what to expect. She decided that she could use her meager savings from her waitressing job to fund her trip. Her excitement grew as the date of their departure approached.

That trip through Europe opened Ginny's eyes in so many ways. When she didn't know how to speak the local language, she learned how to communicate through smiles and hand gestures. She got comfortable dealing with multiple currencies and found that she got quite good at it. She was astonished to discover how easy it was to meet people and make new friends while traveling. Most importantly, she felt a real sense of freedom.

Ginny and Kate could decide on a whim where they were going to go and what they were going to do. They had Eurail passes so they could jump on the train whenever they wanted. They were able to explore cities and towns throughout England, France, Switzerland, and Italy. They took river boat tours and rented bicycles to explore the countryside. They were free to explore Europe at their own pace.

Occasionally they would amicably split up for an afternoon so they each could do their own thing. Sometimes Ginny would find herself sitting happily on a park bench simply taking in the beauty around her. At other times, she would explore a museum on her own so she could linger when she wanted to and skip sections that didn't appeal to her. It was utter bliss.

After her epic summer in Europe, Ginny returned home and went back to school. She felt forever changed by her trip and discovered that she had more clarity and focus in her life. With renewed energy, she resumed her studies and completed her degree in short order. She landed her dream job as an IT Specialist and started working immediately after graduation. She met Tom through friends at work and they soon started dating. After a whirlwind romance, they decided to get married and had a beautiful wedding ceremony with close family and friends.

When I talked with Ginny, she was in her early 30s, her relationship with Tom was strong, and they had built a good life together. Yet she still found herself feeling vaguely unsettled. They talked about having kids at some point, but she wasn't sure she was ready yet. She had a good job which she found rewarding on most days. She was paid well but felt like she didn't get enough time off from work. She frequently had to respond to work email messages when she was on vacation.

She found herself dreaming of the faraway places that were pictured in the gorgeous stock photos on her screensaver. Sometimes she even lost track of time browsing through travel articles and reading travel blogs. Ginny still remembered vividly how incredibly wonderful she felt that one summer when she was free to travel at her own pace. She longed to experience that feeling of freedom again and she didn't want to wait until retirement. She knew there had to be a way to recapture that feeling and still be a responsible adult. She knew that she wanted to see the world while she was still young and healthy enough to enjoy it.

So I showed Ginny what I'm going to show you. I showed her what it would take to responsibly organize her life so she could take a break from her career. I showed her what it would take to live her dream travel adventure now. And I'm going to show that to you too in the following pages.

CHAPTER ONE
Finding a Better
Way to Travel

For my part, I travel not to go anywhere, but to go.
I travel for travel's sake. The great affair is to move."

ROBERT LOUIS STEVENSON

I remember the excitement of my first plane trip to Walt Disney World when I was four years old. It's perhaps telling that I found the plane ride itself to be the highlight of the trip instead of our visit to the world-famous amusement park. I also recall the thrill of picking up my grandmother at the international terminal of the Philadelphia airport whenever she returned from one of her overseas trips. I loved listening to her as she recounted the highlights of her latest trip while I did my best to picture in my head every scene that she described.

Our family didn't often travel by plane, but I vividly remember each time that we did. More often we traveled by car, and I learned to love that too. When I was in second grade my dad was offered a temporary assignment within his company that took us from our suburban Philadelphia home to Phoenix, Arizona. We all piled into our Chevy Impala station wagon for the cross-country trip. We were a complete family of six by then, with my mom, my dad, my three younger sisters, and me. My dad was positioned behind the wheel while my mom sat in the passenger seat with my baby sister, Susan, on her lap (as was custom in those days). The rest of us were sprawled out on blankets and pillows in the rear of the station wagon with the back seat folded down to give us more space.

Heather, Nancy, and I spent most of our time on that trip with our faces in coloring books, MadLibs, and those activity books where you would discover the answers with a special invisible ink pen. Since we have extended family scattered around the country, my parents had chosen to take our time on the journey to see as many relatives as possible along the way. While my dad took great pains to point out landmarks and features along our route and did his best to attract our interest to the scenes outside with typical road trip games, we preferred our own activities over those that were passing us by and my parents probably thought that many benefits of the trip were lost on us. However, in retrospect, that cross-country road trip was one of the most memorable and impactful experiences of my young life, and it was on that trip that my wanderlust really took hold.

As I grew older, my desire to travel continued to grow with me. Whenever I was playing or doing chores in our backyard, I would stop to look up every time a plane flew overhead. *Where were they going?* I would wonder. I enjoyed imagining the wonderful adventures that the airplane passengers were embarking on.

Whenever I happened to hear about other people's recent travels, I found myself enthralled with their stories. Many of these folks seemed to travel to somewhere warm, such as the Caribbean or Hawaii, and would either go on a cruise or stay at an all-inclusive resort. My grandmother regularly went on organized trips with her church group to places in Europe and the Middle East that I considered really exotic. As I grew to understand prices and money, I came to believe that it was really expensive to travel. It also seemed to me that the only accepted way to travel was via an organized, all-inclusive kind of trip that was taken in short one to two-week bursts. I believed for a long time that travel was something that someone like me could not reasonably afford to do.

When I met my husband, Witt, in 1997, he taught me about another way to travel. He had spent several months backpacking in Europe after college and so many of our first conversations were about that trip. It was amazing to me to discover that he was able to travel for months at a time for very little money. I was also stunned that he traveled to places he had never been before without having a tour guide! How was that possible? Didn't he get lost? How did he know where he was going to stay at night? The whole idea boggled my mind. I wanted to learn more and Witt was happy to explain it all to me.

After we dated for a while, Witt next embarked on a multi-month trip through southeastern Asia. I stayed behind for most of this trip, but we did make arrangements to meet up for a month to travel together in New Zealand. It was my first trip ever outside the US, and I flew to the other side of the globe by myself. Witt's flight was due to arrive two days after mine, so I had to figure out somewhere to stay in Auckland as well as how to arrange transportation there from the airport on my own. I chose to stay in a downtown youth hostel, which worked out great. The staff there gave me ideas on places to visit and so I found it surprisingly easy to spend a whole day sightseeing without having a tour guide. I had a fantastic time and my confidence soared. Once Witt arrived, I was able to show *him* around Auckland. It was a wonderful feeling.

From there, we made a plan. We rented a car and for the next four weeks we independently toured the countryside of both the North and South Islands of New Zealand. We strolled through towns and explored national parks. We stayed in youth hostels along the way. We sea kayaked in

Abel Tasman National Park, hiked in Tongariro National Park, and took ferries to travel between the islands. We even visited the dramatic point on the North Island where the Indian Ocean crashes into the Pacific Ocean. In short, we had an absolute blast. We went where we wanted and when we wanted and would change up our plans whenever it suited us. I now fully understood the lure and the benefits of independent travel and I was hooked.

In the years that followed we did similar one-month independent trips to other places: Peru and Bolivia, Maine (where we were married), France and Switzerland, then Chile and Argentina. While we flew by airplane to each location, once we were there we traveled by bus, on trains, by bicycle, and even did multi-day backpacking trips. I even grew to prefer taking the local buses instead of the tour buses.

In 2003, we took our independent travels to a whole new level. We shipped our car to Southampton, England, and spent one year driving through Europe and Africa. At the time, we had a Land Rover Defender 110 that we equipped with a roof-top tent for sleeping, a small refrigerator to keep our food cold, and a Coleman dual-fuel stove to cook our meals. We drove and camped in 23 countries and visited places that previously had sounded really scary to us. We were pleasantly surprised to discover that our fears had been unfounded and we were astounded by the friendliness and hospitality that we encountered everywhere we went. With one full year of positive travel experiences under our belt, I found that I saw the world very differently than I had before.

When we returned to the US after that trip, I started to realize how much my worldview had changed. Issues that I had considered to be black or white before were suddenly nuanced and complex. Having met people whose lives were affected by the actions of our country had a humbling effect on me. I now realized that there was more than one side to every story, and the news often only reported a very small portion of most stories.

After our return we went back to our former jobs, bought a home, and settled down. In 2009, our family grew by one when our son, Quinn, was born. I enjoyed motherhood immensely, though I seem to recall being waist deep in diapers when I realized that I wanted to travel again. I wanted Quinn to see the world for himself and to understand firsthand that there is more than one way to live a happy life. We soon hatched a plan to travel through the Americas, set a date for our departure, and began our preparations.

Quinn was four years old when we left our Denver home in our camper van and headed north. We drove past the Arctic Circle in Canada and then went west to explore Alaska before returning south. After taking care of some necessary van repairs and reconfigurations in Colorado and California, we drove south into Mexico and on into Central

America. In Panama, we put our van on a cargo ship headed to Cartagena, Colombia, where we reunited with it a few weeks later before we ventured on to explore Colombia, Ecuador, Peru, Bolivia, Chile, Argentina, Paraguay, Brazil, and Uruguay. In all, the three of us traveled in our van for two and a half years before we wrapped up our Pan Am trip, put our camper van on a boat back to the US, and flew home.

From taking each of these trips, I have learned the most effective ways to plan and prepare for extended travel adventures. The circumstances of each trip varied: I have taken long vacations and leaves of absences from work and even quit my job altogether. However, in each case, I had to go through the steps that are in this book to make my travel dream a reality.

I've discovered through my own travels just how safe and wonderful the world really is. The overwhelming friendliness of people everywhere continues to amaze and inspire me. The beauty and grandeur of our world never fails to take my breath away. Yet I had to take that first important step to get out and see the world with an open heart to fully appreciate these discoveries, and those first experiences then inspired me to take bigger and bigger steps as my comfort level grew.

This book will show you the way. You will learn what slow travel is and why it results in richer and more rewarding travel experiences. Then you will learn about my W.O.R.L.D.

within R.E.A.C.H. Process. Gathered from my own experiences, as well as from those of other travelers, I have assembled a list of ten steps to escape the daily grind and live your dream travel adventure. We will follow these steps together throughout this book to create your travel itinerary, develop a plan for your career break, and make the preparations you need to embark on your own travel adventure.

W – Welcome Your Why

Whether you know it or not, you have your own reasons for wanting to travel. Your reasons might pop into your head easily or they might be buried deeper inside of you. Together we will explore what your unique reasons are and get super clear on them. This reason or collection of reasons is your *why*. You will want to embrace your why fully and completely so you can successfully take the remaining steps to make your dream trip a reality.

O – Overcome Your Fears

When it comes to trying anything big and new, fears are bound to surface. This is especially true when it comes to traveling to places that we know little to nothing about. We'll talk about why it's important to take everything you hear about in the news media with a giant grain of salt.

Then, to help you overcome your fears, we will examine better methods to obtain more accurate and up-to-date information for your trip and to successfully keep any vague fears at bay.

R – Rough Out (Chart) Your Route

Sometimes one of the biggest challenges is in deciding where to go. The world is a big place with so many fascinating sights to see. How do you begin to decide which places to visit? We'll delve into some ways that you can narrow the list down to those destinations that most excite you and organize them into a rough itinerary that you can use to begin your trip preparations.

L – Live Large on Less

Once you know where you want to go, you'll next need to determine how much money you'll need for your trip. Together we'll go through several strategies that will enable you to comfortably enjoy your travels while still spending much less money than you might've previously thought. This is also where you start making changes in your life now so you can depart on your trip sooner rather than later.

D – Divulge Your Plans

Often our biggest plans don't actually feel real until we set a date and we share the news with others. Deciding upon who you tell first is just as important as how far in advance you share the news with your employer. You'll want to build your support network early to keep your excitement level high as you continue to move forward with your preparations. You'll also want to be in the best position possible with your coworkers and your employer so you have the widest array of options available for yourself moving forward.

—within—

R – Run Your Life Remotely

Your home affairs will still need to be managed somehow while you are away from your home base. By reducing and eliminating as much overhead in your life as possible, you can minimize the amount of time, effort, and money it will take to manage your home life, regardless of wherever you happen to be in the world.

E – Ensure Your Health

Your health is important and taking some simple precautions can make all the difference in being able to fully enjoy your travels with peace of mind. Accidents and illness can happen anywhere that you are so it is worth it to be prepared in advance so you can rest easy while you are out exploring the world.

A – Assemble Your Kit

Deciding what to take with you can be a challenge anytime you're getting ready for a trip. For an even longer travel adventure, you will only want to carry with you the items that you are most likely to need. Since you can't bring your whole wardrobe, you'll need to reframe your mindset to choose items that will provide the most usefulness with the least amount of hassle.

C – Conquer Your Obstacles

Every path worth taking in life is inevitably laden with numerous roadblocks. Planning your dream travel adventure is no different. Navigating around, over, and through each obstacle proactively will help boost your confidence so you can continue on the path that you were meant to take.

H – Hit the Road

When your departure day arrives, you'll be at an amazing juncture in your life. You will have aligned with your dreams and have boldly made the decision to make them happen. Now the moment that you have dreamed about has finally arrived: the moment when you truly start living your travel dream. Your excitement will be pumping vigorously through your veins as you take this pivotal step through the doorway that stands in front of you.

By following this proven ten-step process, you will be able to transform your travel dreams into concrete actions that you can use to make your dream trip a reality.

I've had the privilege of helping many people plan the details of their dream trip. Whether it is helping them decide where to go, what to pack, or how to prepare, it's always amazing to watch their joy grow as their dreams solidify into tangible plans that they can easily envision and start taking action upon. Even better is receiving email messages from them once they have begun their trip. Nothing beats seeing their pride visible on their smiling faces in their photos at their dream destinations.

Even if your idea of adventure doesn't feel very grand at the moment, you can start from wherever you are now. Maybe you wish that you had started traveling earlier in your life. If so, there's really no point to living in the past, whether or not you have regrets. Today is a new day. In fact, that statement is worth repeating: Today is a new day – and you have the power to design your future. Let's kick start your travel life into gear so you can live it the way you want to from now on.

My goal is to show you the steps to follow so you can take a break from your career to travel slowly and independently. Your trip can take any shape or length that you'd like. Every journey begins with a single step. Let's take that first step together.

CHAPTER TWO
What Is Slow Travel?

"Travel is more than the seeing of sights; it is a change that goes on, deep and permanent, in the ideas of living."

Miriam Beard

S low travel is, in many respects, a very different philosophy from what many of us have come to understand as the usual way to travel. It is not at all about cramming in as many sights as possible in as short amount of time as possible. It's not about visiting eight countries in 14 days. It is also not a contest to see how many landmarks you can check off as you scurry from one to the next. So what is slow travel?

Independent Travel. For starters, slow travel is independent travel. You have the freedom to design and tailor your own trip as you go, based on your whims. You can get off the beaten path, away from the tourist crowds, and explore the countryside. You can take days off to relax, do nothing, or to read a good book. You can decide on the fly to change your plans to take in a nearby outdoor concert or to browse in the local farmer's market. If you want to set a fixed itinerary you can, but you can also choose to change it up based on how well you like a place. Maybe you're relaxing at a private beach and don't want to leave. Why not stay for a few more days? If you're not enjoying where you are and what you're doing, then you can simply move on to something else whenever you'd like.

Travel at Your Own Pace. Slow travel also removes the rush. You stay long enough in one place so that you can really explore an area and get a true sense of it. While you might visit major tourist attractions, you can also take time to pause in between to notice the rhythm and way of life that exists beyond the attractions. By doing so, you have the luxury of looking for the extraordinary in the ordinary. For example, allowing yourself to relax at a sidewalk cafe for an afternoon while taking in the scenes of passersby can give you insights into how ordinary people there live their daily lives, and it just might give you some perspective into how you live your own life back home.

Travel with an Open Heart and Mind. Slow travel reduces your dependency on the guidebook. While you might still use a guidebook to provide an overall starting perspective on a place, it's important to open your heart and mind to the possibilities that are right in front of you. Why not try lunch at the bustling family restaurant across the street? See a sign for a festival this weekend? Why not go? No guidebook can possibly cover everything there is worth doing and the reality is that often the finest gems are the places that few foreigners know about. In fact, the more you venture off on your own, the more likely it is that you will have rewarding experiences. You might find that service is friendlier and the food is tastier in a place that doesn't normally see many tourists. Going to a local concert or festival is something that often can't be planned in advance, so why not take the opportunity when it presents itself? You'll get to experience what the local people do for fun and it will provide memories that you can carry with you forever.

Richer Travel Experiences. With slow travel, you are essentially choosing the quality of experiences over the quantity of places to visit. In fact, I would assert that slow travel provides a much richer travel experience overall. Instead of having a two-dimensional visit where you might only visit the highlights listed in your guidebook and then return to your hotel, you can have a more well-rounded stay where you can experience the sights, smells, tastes, sounds, and vibes. In the process, you'll likely make some friends and gather some personal stories that you will reflect on weeks, months, and years later with a smile.

Connect with Local People and Cultures. Connecting with local people and culture is an important part of slow travel. By being friendly with the people that you meet, and opening yourself up to the possibility of meeting someone new, you can add a new depth to your visit. You can discover what everyday people in a region do as part of their daily life – what they do for work, how they travel around, what they do for fun in the evenings and on weekends, and where they go for vacation with their family. You might even be surprised to find that you end up forging a life-long friendship with someone. It's almost magical to see how striking up a conversation and having an open heart and mind can lead to a delightful change in afternoon plans and long-term friendship.

Communicate in the Local Language. Part of being able to connect with the local people is being able to speak at least some of their language. The more you can communicate in the local language, the more you can learn about and from the people that you meet each day. Having some language knowledge also can increase your overall comfort level while you are in that region.

While it's not necessary, nor practical, to be fluent in a country's language, every bit that you do know adds up in considerable ways. If you can converse with people that you meet along the way, you can talk with them about a wider variety of topics and even ask for their recommendations on places to visit. Taxi drivers, for example, often offer a wealth of information about an area, its culture, and its seasonal events. Some of our favorite travel experiences have come about from following the advice of a local person with whom we struck up a conversation. We've found that approach to be the best way to find the gems that only the locals know about.

You might even get invited to stay in someone's home which can be an amazing experience unto itself. Imagine what it might be like to share a meal with a French, Indian, or Peruvian family in their own home. There are few better ways in my opinion to gain insight into a local culture than sitting around the dinner table and eating together as a guest in someone's home. People tend to feel most comfortable in their own homes, and as their guest, they want you to be comfortable too, so you are sure to have a memorable experience.

At one point in our travels, we were traveling in a small, rather remote, game park in South Africa, when we came upon a couple whose car had broken down on the side of the road. We stopped to see if we could help them and learned that they needed to get their car towed to the nearest service station. As it happened, we were in a position to be able to tow their car with our Land Rover so we offered to take them and their car to the next town. We set up the tow strap, piled into our car, and in the process, we struck up a nice conversation with them. We got along so well that they invited us to visit them at their home in another region of South Africa.

We were planning to head in that direction anyway so we did reach out to them several weeks later when we were traveling near their home town. They invited us for dinner and to stay for the night in their home. They had a beautiful house on a bluff overlooking the ocean where whale sightings are common. We enjoyed a lovely dinner with them that evening and afterward we watched a rugby game on their television where they explained the finer points of the game to us. Later that night, we had a very comfortable sleep in their separate guest house. Over breakfast the next morning, they asked us about our travel plans and we told them about our intention to visit the Stellenbosch wine region next. That's when they told us that they had owned a vineyard themselves and had just sold it to their son and daughter. They offered to arrange a private tour of their vineyard if we were interested. We graciously said yes, and a few days later, their son and daughter gave us a personal tour of their vineyard and offered to let us taste each of their wines. When we asked if we could purchase a couple of cases of wine from them, the new vineyard owners offered to sell the wine to us at cost in gratitude for the help that we'd given to their parents.

When we first met them back at that game park, we had no way to know that helping someone on the side of the road would lead to such an amazing experience, but that's exactly the point. There is no way to know. You simply have to be open to the possibility that something wonderful can happen and trust that everything will work out fine. What we've come to discover is that life has a way of delivering on your expectations.

While it definitely helps when you have a common language, what happens if you don't? Since each language presents its own learning challenges, it is often difficult to know how to speak more than just a few words of some languages. This is especially true if you don't plan to stay in a place for more than a few weeks. However, it is still important to know how to greet people with a smile (good morning, good afternoon, hello, and goodbye), be polite (please and thank you) and to learn the numbers to make money transactions easier. While you might worry about doing it wrong, you're just as likely to be surprised when you see how well your efforts are appreciated.

You also don't necessarily need to know much of the language in advance of your arrival if you plan to take time to learn during your stay. For example, while we did try to learn some Spanish before our travels to Latin America, we found learning along the way was very effective for us. We took one to two weeks of Spanish lessons at a stretch in different towns throughout Mexico and Guatemala. With each lesson, we were able to add to our vocabulary, speaking ability, and comprehension. Plus, we were able to put our lessons into practice as part of our daily life, with trips to the grocery store and dining in restaurants. When we studied Spanish in Guanajuato, Mexico, staying with a local family was part of our immersive learning experience. We ate breakfast and lunch each day with our host family so our meal conversations provided excellent Spanish practice for us. We learned quickly, made some wonderful friends, and had a very enjoyable stay there.

We found learning Portuguese to be much more of a challenge. We'd only planned to be in Brazil for a short time, so we didn't have the luxury of learning much of the language. However, since our son has numerous food allergies, it was important to us that we be able to at least order a meal safely. I made an effort to learn more than just the greetings, numbers, and pleasantries so that I could say phrases like "My son is allergic to...," "Does this contain...?" and "It's very important," and be understood. When it was time for us to leave Brazil, my skills had progressed to the point that I could speak Portuguese in complete sentences when ordering at a restaurant and I could understand some Portuguese words when they were spoken to me.

Even so, there were several situations where we wished we knew more Portuguese. We met one family in particular that struck up a conversation with us. As hard as we tried, our conversation was naturally limited to our knowledge of their language. I'm pretty confident that our conversation could've led to something even more wonderful had we been able to converse better with them. Making an effort to learn the language is one of those activities where the benefits are tangible and well worth it.

Travel Overland. Another important component of slow travel is that it involves a higher percentage of time on the ground and traveling "overland" than in airplanes. Overland (or overwater) travel can include traveling by trains, buses, motorcycles, bicycles, taxis, cars, boats, campers, horseback, etc. It can be via public transportation, in your own vehicle, or you can hire/rent a vehicle. It can also be a mixture of all sorts of transportation methods.

There are several benefits to traveling overland. For starters, it's easier to see how the landscapes change as you travel. You can see how the climate, the flora, and the fauna change with elevation and with distance, as you travel from the jungle to the mountains to the desert and to the ocean. You can also see and interact with other people more easily, so you naturally have more opportunities to create memorable experiences. Another benefit is that you can get away from the tourist crowds and visit smaller towns where the locals are happy to see you, tend to be friendlier toward you, and often want to know more about you. You can also find beautiful, secluded beaches, and fantastic family restaurants where the food is unlike anything you've ever had.

Travel as a Lifestyle. The final, and perhaps most important, point about slow travel is that it is not a vacation. Instead, it is living your life differently. On a vacation, it's common to stay in hotels and eat out in restaurants for every meal. You might even bring enough clothes to last for your entire trip without having to do laundry until you get home. In short, being on vacation is more of an escape from life and bears few of the normal components of home life.

Slow travel by necessity includes many aspects of life at home. You will still have to do life maintenance tasks, such as doing laundry (or paying someone to do it for you), buying groceries, and making meals. That's not to say you won't be eating out, because you probably will. You just probably won't be eating out for every meal on every day of your trip. This is actually a huge benefit because it not only reduces your overall expenses, but it also helps to stave off homesickness. We've discovered that one of the single biggest causes of homesickness is missing the food from home. Buying your own groceries and preparing your own meals means that you can make your own favorite dishes whenever you want to. Even if you consider yourself to be an adventurous eater, most people have their limits, especially when it comes to breakfast. You might be traveling in Japan, for example, and discover that eating fish first thing in the morning just doesn't appeal to you. With slow travel, that's easily solved with a trip to the grocery store where you can find the ingredients to make omelets or pancakes that you could whip up in the kitchen of your rental home or hostel.

In summary, slow travel eliminates the rush, is independent, and selects quality experiences over always following a guidebook. The deeper the experience, the richer the memories will be. Slow travel also means making connections with local people and their culture, communicating in the regional language, and spending the majority of time traveling overland. Slow travel is more than a vacation; it is life differently. Slow travel can provide you with rich experiences and unforgettable memories. Once you get a taste of it, you'll likely be hooked too.

Stepping Boldly Forward

1. Think back to your last vacation. Where did you go and what did you do? Which activities involved leaving your comfort zone? How did that feel?

2. What kind of memories do you have from this trip? Which stories do you like to share with others? Identify which elements of your travel experience contribute to making it a story worth sharing.

3. Which kinds of stories from books and movies do you find most fascinating? Is there an element of challenge or risk? Was there an unexpected ending? Consider for a moment how slow travel could offer you the opportunity to have richer life experiences.

CHAPTER THREE
Why Go?

*"Twenty years from now you will be more disappointed
by the things you didn't do than by the ones you
did do. So throw off the bowlines, sail away from
the safe harbor. Catch the trade winds in
your sails. Explore. Dream. Discover."*

MARK TWAIN

Step One: Welcome Your Why

You might question why it's worth taking a trip longer than a vacation and why it's a good idea to go now instead of waiting until later. Surely you'll have plenty of time to travel later on, right? And it is true that it's possible to pack quite a lot of travel activities into a two to three-week vacation. Nevertheless, I can offer many reasons to take a career break / mini-retirement so you can slow travel now.

Reach More Destination Options. For starters, some things just don't fit into a two-week vacation. Perhaps you want to travel to somewhere on the other side of the globe, like the Great Wall of China, for example. Even if you only take into account the travel time to get there and back you're looking at spending about one to two days on each end of your trip just to arrive in the country. You'll then need a few days to recover from the substantial jet lag that you're likely to experience from suddenly having your days and nights switched. By the time you factor the travel and recovery time in, you're left with only about one week to explore the vast country of China. With the amount of travel time required as well as the significant cost to fly there, is one week really enough time to even make that trip worth it to you? You'd scarcely be there and it'll be almost time to come home. With a few more weeks, however, you could have a lot more freedom, add a couple more places to your itinerary, and really slow down to enjoy yourself. You could turn a fast-paced jaunt around the world into a life-changing experience that you will fondly remember forever.

Check Off Bucket List Items. Taking your mini-retirement to travel is also an opportunity to cross off some bucket list items that may be harder to do later in life. Maybe you'd really like to hike the Inca Trail to Machu Picchu. As one of the most visited places in South America, it is on many people's short list of places to see. This is for good reason as it is a stunning experience and it's well worth the trip. However, the hike on the trail is not considered to be an easy walk and should not be underestimated. There are three high mountain passes on the trail that you need to cross and the trail is largely made up of carefully arranged rocks, making it a little tougher on our knees and ankles than a normal dirt trail. It helps that you'll have a guide and some porters to carry most of your gear and your food (as it's required by law), so you won't have heavy packs to contend with. Nevertheless, you'll want to be in decent physical shape to make the trip enjoyable. For most of us, we're more likely to be in better shape now than we will be in 20, 30, or 40 years. We might not even be able to do this hike at all if we wait until later in life. By going while you are in good physical health, you can have the experience that you dream of while you still can.

Your Future is Unpredictable. You also don't have a crystal ball to see into your future. Not only could your own health change, but the health of your family members could change as well. It's definitely harder to break away to travel if you have a sick parent, spouse, or other family member who needs you to be nearby to help. It is much better for your own peace of mind to make travel a priority while you don't have loved ones at home depending on you for their care.

In addition, your financial situation could change significantly in the future from what it is now. We all like to think that our financial future will be better than our current situation, and hopefully it will be. Yet it is one of the hallmarks of our existence that there are few guarantees in life. Markets regularly rise and fall, and economies respond in kind.

For example, the housing slump in 2008 was the single biggest factor that prevented my husband and me from taking a year-long break to go to Kenya. We couldn't sell or rent our townhouse without taking a significant financial loss, so we made the difficult decision to turn down an exciting opportunity to volunteer with Voluntary Service Overseas [VSO] (which is a Canadian organization similar to the US Peace Corps). We were very disappointed that the timing did not work out in our favor, especially after the months of training and preparation that we'd undertaken. Then life threw another curve ball our way. About six months after we declined that opportunity, we discovered that we were soon to become parents, and from there our lives went in a whole new direction. In the years that followed, we were still able to figure out ways to travel the world with our son. However, because VSO has a policy of not allowing kids to go along on assignments to developing countries, this particular opportunity was no longer available to us.

Deepen and Strengthen Your Marriage. When traveling with your partner or spouse, taking a long break to slow travel gives you the chance to spend quality time together. Instead of heading off in different directions each day to go to work, you get to spend your days together while traveling. Your trip can be a wonderful opportunity to strengthen and deepen your relationship with each other.

When traveling with a partner you will likely see the best (and worst) sides of each other at various times of your trip. By working through these ups and downs together, you get to discover and appreciate how resilient and resourceful each of you can be.

Bond with Your Kids. This is also true when traveling with your kids. While conventional wisdom might say that it's better to wait until your kids are older to travel, we know many other traveling families who have found the exact opposite to be true. There are some types of travel that are easier to do while your kids are younger, while they are more portable, and while they still like hanging out with you. Your time together exploring other countries and cultures can bring you together quickly and more effectively than other kinds of situations. Best of all, you'll get to build beautiful memories together that you can reflect on fondly and share stories about for years.

Become the Adventurer You've Always Wanted to Be. Taking a long break to slow travel also provides you with an opportunity to unleash your inner adventurer. It is said that growth only happens outside your comfort zone and slow travel offers plenty of opportunities to get outside of yours. By taking the time for a mini-retirement now, you can more effectively capitalize on your personal growth to become the person that you've always wanted to be – and do so while you're still young enough to be able to do something about it. Also, think about all the stories you'll be able to share with your grandkids someday. You'll be the coolest grandma on the block!

Volunteer Your Time and Skills. Perhaps you'd really like to have some time to do some volunteer work. Using your mini-retirement to slow travel can provide an opportunity to contribute your skills in a meaningful way to a community. There are thousands of organizations where you could volunteer your time in locations all around the world. You can select an organization that respects indigenous cultures, cares about the long-term benefit of the community, and makes it a top priority to empower local people effectively.

There are many excellent reasons to travel. It's super important that you are clear on your reason and that this purpose is deep and personal to you. You don't ever need to explain your specific reasons to anyone else if you don't want to. But you do need to know the reason in your heart and be committed to figuring out a way to achieve it. This is how you make your dreams come true, and this is the key to making your mini-retirement a reality.

Stepping Boldly Forward

1. Why do you want to travel? What benefit(s) do you hope to gain from changing things up? What will happen to you if you don't take this break?

2. What are the reasons that you feel inspired to travel? What is your top reason for wanting to get out and see the world? Write it down as soon as it comes to you. How do you think you will feel if you don't follow your inspiration?

3. If you could choose the perfect time to take your dream trip, when would that be? Picture in your mind how old you will be when you are visiting your dream destinations. What types of activities do you envision yourself doing while you're visiting each place? How far into the future will you be traveling and how old will you be?

CHAPTER FOUR
Is It Safe?

"A ship in harbor is safe, but that is not
what ships are built for."

JOHN A. SHEDD

Step Two: Overcome Your Fears

The idea of going to places that are largely unknown to us can be scary. We might feel a little better about going to a place if someone we know has been there and had a great time. More often than not, though, we may have formed negative impressions of a place at some point and not really know why. Or we may have heard about something specific happening in a region, probably from reading or listening to the news.

It's Safer Than You Think. Let me start by telling you that I've found the people that I've met in my travels to be consistently wonderful. Like most people, I was a nervous traveler when I first started out. As enthusiastic as I was about the idea of traveling, when it really came down to it, I had difficulty reconciling that enthusiasm with what I had come to understand about the world from the news sources available to me. Once I started to travel, however, I learned that the reality on the ground was often much different from what I had been led to believe.

When we arrived in Morocco in early 2004 near the beginning of our yearlong Africa trip, I was very nervous about traveling in Muslim countries and my fear was palpable. I recall walking late one afternoon with my husband by one of the local teahouses. Visible through the big windows of the teahouse, a speech by our US President was being rebroadcast on the TV. While the Arabic subtitles on the screen enabled those watching to understand what was being said in their native language, we could clearly understand the President's spoken words. The content was famously known as the "Axis of Evil" speech, and here it was being played loudly in English in a teahouse filled with Muslim men. We wondered what on earth the men in the tea house were thinking as they watched. Had the US declared war on an entire religion? We didn't know what to make of it all. We especially didn't know what it meant for us and for our safety. After all, we were traveling in a Muslim country with US passports. We felt for sure that this event did not bode well for us and our travel plans.

We soon learned, however, that our fears were unfounded. We came to understand later that most people in the world do not attribute the actions of a leader to its citizens. Nevertheless, our nerves were rattled after this experience.

While in Morocco, we needed to replace one of the tires on our Land Rover. We'd had a blow out while we were driving on the highway a few days before and needed a new spare tire. We pulled into a fuel station in Casablanca where we inquired in broken French about where we could purchase tires nearby. After a few minutes, a well-dressed business man walked up to us and asked us in perfect English how he could help us. We explained to him what we needed and he offered to take us to a place where we could buy a suitable tire.

He climbed into his late-model Mercedes and instructed us to follow him. We drove behind him through the narrow city streets until we arrived at a nondescript building. When we got out of our car, he called over to a young boy, gave him a few dirhams and asked him to watch both of our cars. We went inside the shop, which did indeed have tires for sale, but we were very disappointed by the selection and quality of tires available. Our new friend told us not to worry, we will go to another shop. He also emphasized to us that we should only buy if we are happy with the purchase.

So we followed him to another shop, then another, and another. Not one of these shops had any tires that were in good enough condition to take us long distances on bad roads and in deep sand.

Our well-mannered friend ended up spending that whole day with us. Throughout the day, we heard him talking on his cell phone as he canceled and rescheduled the meetings that he was missing. It seemed crazy to us that he would go to these lengths just to lead us around town in fruitless pursuit of automobile tires.

We were completely dumbfounded. Why would he give up his entire work day to help us? While the situation made absolutely no sense to us, we were deeply grateful for his help.

When we finally parted ways at the end of the day, we thanked him for taking time out of his busy day. We also took that opportunity to ask him why he decided to help us. I don't think that I will ever forget his thoughtful answer.

He replied, "In the Koran, it says we must help three groups of people: family, friends and those 'who know no one.' You are travelers and know no one here, and that is why I helped you."

In the span of that one day, we went from being afraid of what might happen to us while traveling in a Muslim country, to being utterly blown away by the kindness of a

Muslim businessman. This was the first time we'd discovered that our preconceived notions were misplaced, but it was definitely not the last.

Keep News in Perspective. What we've come to understand is that, in general, newspapers and news programs only cover the worst events of any place. The financial viability of nearly every newspaper company is driven by sales. The more sensational and dramatic the news stories are, the more likely it is that someone will purchase a copy of the daily newspaper. There's also another interesting human tendency that comes into play. When we read stories about a place we know little about, we tend to associate that one event in our minds to a much larger region than where the localized event took place. This can mean that we mentally tie an event that occurs in a very specific region with the level of safety of an entire country, or sometimes an entire continent.

I recall a conversation that I had while getting my hair cut in Johannesburg toward the end of our Africa trip. As I was sitting in the chair at the salon, the stylist noticed my accent and asked me where I was from. When I told her that I was from the US, she told me she had always wanted to visit the US but she was afraid to go there because of the rampant crime. I was stunned. The thing is, Jo'burg isn't exactly known for its low crime rate. It was tough for me to understand why she thought there would be more crime in the US. I mean, the US is safe, right? So I asked her for more information. What kind of crime was she referring to? It turns out that she had heard about some drive-by shootings in Florida from the news and had assumed it was a problem throughout the entire US.

When it comes to our home environment, we all know how to compartmentalize and even minimize risks because our experience tells us it's unlikely to happen to us. We tell ourselves that we are safe because we don't live in Florida, because we don't drive deserted roads late at night, or whatever the reason. But when something happens somewhere else, especially somewhere we are unfamiliar with, we tend to blow the risk out of proportion. When Ebola broke out a few years ago in a small western African country, many people canceled their trips to game parks in eastern and southern Africa. It didn't matter that Africa is three times the size of the continental US – what happened in one tiny region in Africa was presumed to affect the entire continent of Africa.

Every one of us is susceptible to news stories to some extent. Even after having a fantastic time during our Africa trip, we found ourselves facing our fears again ten years later when we were preparing to travel into Mexico with our young son. We'd heard lots of terrible stories in the news, and it was only after doing some research to determine where exactly those incidents had happened and how we could minimize our risk that we felt comfortable proceeding with our travel plans.

I'm so glad we did. Our time in Mexico turned out to be one of the biggest highlights of any of our trips and Mexico came to be one of our favorite countries overall. We had planned to only stay three months in the country yet we ended up staying six months. The food was fantastic, the people were incredibly friendly, and the cultures and history throughout Mexico were diverse and intriguing. Moreover, Mexico turned out to be even more family-friendly than most other places we'd been, including the US. It saddens me to realize that we would have missed out on all of that if we had let our fears prevent us from traveling into Mexico.

The truth is that bad things can happen to you no matter where you are. The Aurora theater shooting occurred just one mile down the street from my office at the time and less than five miles from my home. I still remember seeing all the news vans and ambulances at the hospital when I was driving to work that next morning. With shooting events like that one becoming more of a regular occurrence in our society, how can we really feel that the danger is worse elsewhere?

Some Things Are Just Random. There is probably nothing we can really do to protect ourselves from random acts of violence, since they are, by their very nature, random. Accidents, too, can happen anywhere. Most car accidents happen within a ten-mile radius of our home (because that's where we tend to drive the most) and they often happen while we are driving to and from work or taking care of errands that we do on a routine basis. Even if we were to stay home all the time in an effort to protect ourselves, it wouldn't guarantee that we won't fall in the bathtub or accidentally get injured in some other way. Besides, living in a bubble, even a self-imposed bubble, is really no way to live.

So I think it comes down to the question: Do you want to live your life in fear, or are you willing to take on a reasonable amount of risk so you can live a fantastic life? Personally, I vote for living a fantastic life – mainly because it's a lot more fun and fulfilling. I also don't want to look back on my life with regrets about things that I really wanted to do but didn't because I feared what might happen. As long as my dream is bigger than my fear, I will figure out a safe and responsible way to make my travel dreams happen.

Take Calculated Risks. That's not to say that I advocate for taking risk just for risk's sake, or for going into a situation blindly. I don't. Instead I recommend that you take calculated and manageable risks. Usually all it takes is doing a little research about where you plan to go to gain a reasonable understanding of the risks and figure out how you might mitigate or avoid them altogether. By being armed with specific knowledge about where you plan to visit, it is much easier to plan and prepare for any situation. In addition, by having access to relevant information for a specific region, you will likely find that your overall fear will subside.

Arm Yourself with Specific Information. The best approach that I have found to learn about what a particular place is really like is to talk with other travelers who have recently been specifically where you want to go. Every city and region is different, so the more specific you can be in your search for information, the more accurate your results will be. With the availability of the internet and social networking, this is quite easy to do. There are hundreds, if not thousands, of travel groups on Facebook, for example, that have been created to exchange this kind of information. It's worth it to join a few of these types of groups while you are still in the planning stages so you can get a sense of the kind of information that is typically shared in each group before you start posting your own questions.

You can also talk with people that you encounter in your daily life. Do you know someone who travels a lot for fun and has recently been to where you want to go? Ask them about their travels and what their highlights were in the place you want to visit. The important point to remember is to find out specifically where they went and figure out how that compares with where you plan to go. Even places in relatively close proximity can be very different. If you were going to Disneyland in California, for example, and someone you know just came from south central Los Angeles, you might reconsider your trip if you mistook your friend's experiences for what you might encounter in Disneyland. That's why it's really important to ask for specifics and take the information you receive in the context it is given.

Once you start your trip, you are likely to encounter other travelers who have visited some of the places that are on your itinerary. Experienced travelers tend to enjoy exchanging travel stories and advice with each other and you'll find that it's often the main topic of conversation whenever two or more travelers are gathered together. The best advice tends to come from those who have the most travel experience, because they are able to compare their own experiences from different places and put them into perspective for you.

It's important to remember not to let vague fears stop you from going after your travel dreams. It is said that courage is not the absence of fear, but the triumph over it. Pinpoint what exactly you are afraid could happen and do a little digging to learn more specifics about places that you want to visit. When you have solid, reliable information at your disposal, you will feel more in control and your fears are likely to subside.

Stepping Boldly Forward

1. Take some time to reflect on what types of situations tend to raise your fears. Really dig deep and be honest with yourself. Write down everything that comes to mind. Consider the kinds of preparation that you could do to manage your fears.

2. Search Facebook for travel groups that interest you and select a few to join. Observe the ongoing conversations to learn more about the kinds of topics that come up for other travelers.

3. If you have specific destinations in mind, post some questions on one of the Facebook groups. You could find out who has recently been to that destination and then ask them about the highlights of their trip. Ask them if they have any specific suggestions for someone who plans to visit there in the future.

CHAPTER FIVE
Deciding Where to Go

*"One's destination is never a place, but a
new way of seeing things."*

HENRY MILLER

Step Three: Rough out (Chart) Your Route

D eciding where to visit on your trip might be one
of the biggest challenges for you. Then again, it
might not. It's often easy to come up with a list
of places that you want to see. However, narrow-
ing the list down and focusing on what exactly your
top priorities are can be more daunting. Our planet is big and
diverse, so the possibilities are endless. How on Earth could
you possibly choose?

Review Your Bucket List. A good place to start is to
first figure out which places are on your bucket list. Close

your eyes and search your heart. Which major landmarks do you want to see? Is there someplace in particular that has always called your name? Maybe there's an experience that you've always dreamed of, such as: watching the sun rise over Machu Picchu, viewing Paris at night from the Eiffel Tower, scuba diving at the Great Barrier Reef, watching elephants play at a watering hole while on safari, feeling the grandeur of the Himalayan mountains, or observing the magical colors of the Northern Lights.

It's important to identify at least one place from your bucket list. Whichever place (or places) you decide on, you should ideally be bursting with excitement about going there. How will it feel for you to be there and experience it for yourself? Perhaps you already feel the excitement welling up inside of you. Do you wish you could just transport yourself there now? If you don't visit your chosen place and experience it on your trip, will you end up regretting it? The answers to these questions can help you select your top place to visit. Ponder it until you know you've found it. This is your number one priority when putting together your itinerary. If your spouse will be going with you, be sure to include him in this process so that you both can benefit.

Follow Your Bliss. You'll also want to consider which kinds of places you'd like to visit in general. Are you a fan of beaches or mountains? Do you prefer lingering in museums or art galleries? Would you like to take cooking classes to really experience a local culture? Or perhaps you would love to unleash your inner Indiana Jones while exploring archeological monuments? Which types of experiences appeal to you most?

You can also choose to have your trip be more activity-focused. Perhaps you love to hike, rock climb, bike, scuba dive, ski, or do yoga. You could focus part of your trip around participating in activities that you love. Your activity could even serve as a theme for your trip. You could identify some of the top places in the world for rock climbing or hiking, for example, and make the most of your trip by going to each of those places to experience them firsthand. You can, of course, see and do other activities and visit other sights along the way, and I highly recommend that you do so. Centering your trip around your favorite activity simply provides a fun framework around which the rest of your trip can be built.

Connect with Loved Ones. Another factor to consider is whether you have friends or family that live in other countries. If so, you may want to make it a priority to visit them while you are in traveling mode. You might be able to stay with them in their home, share meals with them, and get their advice on what to see and do while you are there. They might even offer to take you to their favorite places themselves. In my opinion, being able to stay with friends or family while abroad is an opportunity that can have significant rewards. It can also be an economical option for a while, but you'll want to do what you can to ensure that you are being a good houseguest so you don't risk wearing out your welcome.

Delve into Your Heritage. Similarly, maybe you'd love to take this opportunity to explore your heritage. You can dive into the history of your ancestors' homeland and look up long-lost relatives to help round out your family tree. You could take dance classes or cooking lessons while there so you can bring a bit of your heritage back home with you. Visiting your ancestors' homeland can also provide an extra special opportunity to participate in local festivals and get a deeper sense of the customs there. Some examples include: Oktoberfest in Bavaria, the Running of the Bulls in Barcelona, and the Day of the Dead (El Día de los Muertos) in Mexico. Having a personal connection will enable you to feel the energy on a deeper level as you immerse yourself in the sights, the sounds, and the tastes while participating in these types of activities. You'll also carry these experiences with you long afterward as part of your newly enriched identity.

Contribute to Communities. Perhaps you'd prefer to do some volunteer work instead. Your trip can serve as a wonderful chance to offer your skills and expertise to communities that could really benefit from them. There are many non-profit organizations around the world from which to choose and it's important to do your homework first. Since you'll likely want your impact to be both tangible and sustainable, you'll want to be sure that the organization with which you will be working will leverage your efforts for the long-term benefit of the community. It's an unfortunate reality that some organizations, even with the best of intentions, can inadvertently cause more harm than good to the communities they help. For example, there's often no need for foreigners to come in and build houses since the local people in those communities often have in-depth experience in these highly-skilled fields.

One volunteer organization that I highly recommend is *Do Good as You Go*. They partner with non-profit organizations that are well-established in local communities to identify real needs and match those needs with the skill sets and travel plans of selected volunteers. As a traveler, you have peace of mind knowing that your time and skills are greatly valued since the local organization lays the groundwork for your visit before your arrival and ensures that the community continues to benefit from your visit long after your departure. Do Good as You Go has partners in countries around the globe, so the odds are good that they will have locations near some of your desired destinations.

List Your Destinations. Hopefully, by this point, you've already identified a bunch of places that you want to visit. Now it's time to take stock of what you have thus far. You can start by compiling a list of all the places where you want to go. Then prioritize the destinations on your list in rough order from those most important to those least important to you. Next, you can group the sights by geographic region, since it may be fairly easy to combine multiple places into one visit to a region. Ideally, you'll want to spend approximately one to three months in each region that you have listed to get the most out of your travels. Depending upon how many places you have on your list and how much travel time you have for this trip, you may find that you need to postpone some of the entries toward the bottom of the list for a later trip.

Determine Visa Requirements. From the regions you have listed, figure out which individual countries will be included in your travels. Each country has its own visa requirements for tourists and you should check what the visa requirements are for someone traveling from your passport country. You may find that a 90-day visa is automatically issued upon entry to someone traveling under your country's passport. This is the easiest situation as you can simply show up at the border or airport, your passport will be stamped, and you're good to go for the duration of the visa. In other cases, you may have to visit an embassy for that country (or send your passport away to that country's embassy) in order to apply for your visa in advance of your visit. Fees are usually involved when applying for a visa and they can be pricey in some cases. The main point here is to be aware of whether you'll need to arrange for visas in advance so you can take that into account during the planning process.

Decide When to Visit Each Destination. So now you've got your prioritized list of destinations and countries.

You've also now got an understanding of the visa requirements for each place on your list. The next step is to figure out if there's a particular time of year that you would like to visit each place. In some cases, this will be easy to determine. For example, if it's your dream to visit Paris in the springtime then you'll want to be there sometime between April and June. The best time to see the northern lights is during the winter months when it is dark most of the time, so that would be sometime between November and March.

In other cases, you might want to avoid the extreme weather and temperatures that tend to occur in certain seasons of the year. For example, you might prefer to visit the Taj Mahal and other tropical destinations when it's not in the middle of the monsoon season and also when it's not oppressively hot. You may prefer warmer temperatures over colder temperatures. The criteria for timing your visits can also vary from place to place and can depend on the goals of your visit.

Another set of factors to take into account is the timing of peak season, holidays, and any special events (such as the Olympics or the World Cup) in each location. While peak season may be considered the most desirable time to visit a popular location, it is also when you may have to contend with crowds, higher prices, and a bit more difficulty in finding suitable accommodations. Visiting during the "shoulder season" can be a good way to visit a popular place as that's when the weather conditions are likely to be closer to ideal, the prices tend to be lower, and the crowds are usually less of a factor. Some people even enjoy traveling during the off season because they find it to be a more pleasant experience. It all comes down to what kinds of experiences you prefer.

Create Your Rough Itinerary. By taking the seasons into account, you can now begin to order your destinations by time frame so that you have a rough itinerary for your trip. Next, briefly consider how you might get from one of your destinations to another. For example, you may be able to take a train, bus, or boat between areas that are in reasonably close proximity to each other. When covering longer distances, particularly when traveling over oceans or between continents, air travel may be the most logical way to go. For each leg of your trip you can pencil in which mode(s) of transportation you would prefer to use to travel between your chosen destinations. Though your transportation details may change as your plans solidify further, this is a good starting point.

You now have a rough itinerary for your trip. You've identified your must-see destinations, determined which activities you'd like to include, and decided on a theme or goal to tie the pieces of your trip together. You've prioritized your list of chosen destinations and figured out the ideal time of year when you would like to visit each region. You've organized your destinations into rough chronological order and you've given some thought as to how you might travel between regions.

Create Your Travel Vision Board. By now, a clear picture is emerging for you. To make your dream trip even more real, I recommend that you put together a collection of photos of the places you have included in your itinerary. You can browse through photos on the internet to find those that you find most inspiring. Pinterest and Instagram are great sources of beautiful travel photos that you can use to create your own personal collection that will stoke your enthusiasm as you prepare for your departure. In addition to including pictures of stunning landscapes, it's helpful to find photos that portray the types of activities you plan to participate in. You can also add inspirational quotes or phrases that help get your mojo going.

Collect and arrange your inspirational materials together into a beautiful collage or vision board and then hang your creation up in a place where you can see it several times per day. Every time you see the collage, it will raise up emotions of excitement, possibility, and maybe even some butterflies. If so, you're in the right state of mind. This is your future. You've now taken your first step on your journey. Congratulations!

Now it's time to plan the next piece of your travel adventure. Stay with me. You've got this.

Stepping Boldly Forward

1. Which destinations are high on your bucket list? You can search travel websites and blogs for inspiration. Which places fill you with excitement and wonder? Write them down as you think of them.

2. Do you envision a particular theme that could provide a framework for your itinerary? Your theme could be based on your activities and passions, your personal connections, or your heritage.

3. Determine which seasons of the year would be ideal for your visit to each of your desired destinations.

4. Organize your destinations into rough chronological order based on the seasons that you chose. Identify any destinations that could be loosely grouped together into one region. Give some thought as to how you would prefer to travel between regions.

5. Create a collage or vision board that you can use to keep your excitement high while you prepare for your departure.

CHAPTER SIX
Affording Your Dream Trip

"The world only exists in your eyes.... You can make it as big or as small as you want it."

F. Scott Fitzgerald

Step Four: Live Large on Less

Y ou might now be asking yourself, "But how can I afford it?" When we think about taking any kind of trip, this is often one of the first questions that we ask ourselves, and for good reason. Often, we associate travel with indulging in expensive vacation packages or itineraries. For many of us, we usually only have one to two weeks off from work when we're on vacation, so we're often willing to splurge a bit to make the most of our limited time away. We'll stay at higher-end hotels and resorts because of the amenities that are easily available to us there. Eating out tends to be the norm and we're likely to spring for a gourmet dining experience or two if it is available. If we stay in an all-inclusive resort, we do so because of convenience so we never have to visit a grocery store, spend time on food preparation and cleanup, and because an attentive staff is on-hand to attend to our every need.

We also may associate travel with images of the rich and famous luxuriating on yachts and on fancy beaches. The ultra-rich spare no expense when traveling, and they usually don't have to. It's just the way they travel in those circles. If you happen to have the resources to travel in opulent luxury and want to do that, well then by all means, go for it. For the rest of us mortals, there are lots of other ways to travel comfortably without breaking the bank. Let's look at some approaches that will enable you to dramatically reduce some of the usual travel expenses.

Reduce Daily Cost by Extending Your Travel Time. As I've already mentioned, one key way that slow travel differs from a typical vacation is the time element. Having more time to travel means that you don't need to cram a crazy number of experiences into just one or two weeks. In fact, that model doesn't usually scale up easily when you expand it beyond the usual vacation time frame. Even if you did try to jam-pack travel activities into a span of one to two *months*, for example, you would probably either burn out from trying to keep up with that travel pace, or you would quickly run out of money, or both.

The more that you lengthen the period of time for your trip and slow your travel place down, the more affordable your trip can be. This may sound like a contradiction, but it's really not. Often one of the biggest elements of a vacation is the transportation to get to and from your destination. When you figure in the average cost per day for a short vacation, these transportation expenses can be a significant factor in your average daily cost. Conversely, when you travel for longer periods of time, your transportation costs end up being a less significant factor overall.

Book Lodging by the Month. As I mentioned before, slow travel is not a vacation. Instead, slow travel provides the freedom and opportunity to live life without many of the usual life restrictions. While you might still occasionally stay in hotels when slow traveling, it's usually more of an occasional splurge instead of a daily expense. There are many affordable options for accommodations once you extend your stay in an area to a period of months instead of weeks. You may already be familiar with companies like Airbnb and VRBO that allow for rental of home-like accommodations throughout the world. While renting a home or apartment for a week can be less expensive than paying for a hotel, the average daily cost tends to plummet once you sign up for a month or longer in one place. Since you'll also have access to a kitchen, you can also save significant expense by preparing your own meals most of the time. This practice not only helps to stave off homesickness, but it also gives you more resources to direct toward dining out when the mood strikes you.

Help Out at a Homestay. Another option for inexpensive travel accommodations is through a homestay. A homestay provides comfortable accommodations for little to no charge in exchange for spending a few hours per week helping the owners out with pre-negotiated tasks. The details of each experience can vary quite a bit, but you can often get a decent idea by exploring some of the opportunities available on homestay websites.

Do a Home Exchange. There are also websites where you can arrange to exchange your home with someone else's in your chosen destination. Usually these are an even trade of accommodations for a period of time. The owner still pays all of their home expenses and stays for free in their away accommodations. This type of arrangement often works really well because both parties involved are home owners with an investment on the line, so there is a level of mutual respect and care of property present at all times.

Housesit at Your Destination. With housesitting, you get to take care of someone else's home (and sometimes their pets too) while the homeowners are away. The details can vary with every situation and are best when pre-negotiated prior to arrival. Finding a house-sit can depend on where you choose to go, but it's a fairly common practice in some parts of the world. When you do find a place to house-sit in your chosen destination, you've essentially landed a new home base from which you can explore that region and get a real sense of what it would be like to live there.

Bring Your RV or Camper. One of my favorite modes of travel is with a camper, mainly because we get to bring our home with us. Our family has traveled through four continents this way and it is fabulous. You can bring your bed and your kitchen with you so your food and lodging costs become much smaller. In addition, you've got ready-made transportation as part of the package. Smaller-sized campers are definitely more practical when it comes to traveling internationally because it saves on tolls, parking, fuel, and they are much easier to handle logistically. It's hard to beat being able to drive to a secluded beach and camp there for as long as you want.

Opt for Hostels. Hotels and hostels are always available when you need a place to stay for shorter periods of time. Hotels are great for an occasional splurge, while hostels can be a good, affordable option, especially when staying in expensive cities. While some hostels got their start by catering to the young backpacker set, most have expanded to be more broadly inclusive. Many hostels offer private rooms that are ideal for couples or families and it's common for some of these rooms to offer the option of a private bathroom. Most hostels have instituted a noise curfew, so you don't have to worry about any late-night parties interfering with a good night's sleep. Hostels usually offer an abundance of information about the surrounding area, and you can also learn a lot by talking with other travelers in the common room. Every traveler will have their own opinions, so you'll want to take each bit of information you receive in that context. By talking to many different travelers about a subject or a place, a clear picture will start to emerge. You will likely get some invaluable travel tips as well as some fantastic ideas of where you might want to go next.

Reduce Your Home Expenses. Reducing or eliminating your home expenses will be the biggest factor in being able to afford long-term travel. When you go on vacation, you typically still pay your home expenses such as your rent or mortgage, your utilities, and your gym membership. When you travel for a longer period of time, you will want to do what you can to reduce or eliminate as many of these kinds of expenses as you can. If you haven't yet calculated how much money you spend per month at home, now is a good time to get a handle on that. The magnitude of the numbers may surprise you. That's why – when you plan to be away for six months, one year, or longer – it makes sense to sell or rent out your place to cover your expenses during your absence. The closer you can get your home expenses to zero, the longer you will be able to afford to travel.

Estimate Your Daily Rate. Next, you'll want to estimate how much you'll need to save for your trip. The amount that you need will likely vary depending on where you want to go and what kinds of activities you want to do, but it's probably going to be less than you might think. For our year-long trip through Africa, for example, we spent on average about $50 per day for two of us. That amount covered everything: transportation costs, visa expenses, groceries, eating out, lodging, sightseeing, etc. While our actual expenses varied day to day from that average, it ended up working out overall. For our trip through the Americas ten years later, our costs were higher. For a family of three, we spent on average about $100 per day, and that included some big-ticket items such as a week-long sailing cruise in the Galapagos. In both cases we lived comfortably, we ate out at nice restaurants when we wanted, and we splurged on sightseeing activities when we desired.

To figure out how much you'll need, you can start by estimating the cost of airline tickets as well as the approximate price of any big-ticket tours that you plan to take. Some quick searches on the internet can give you some ballpark numbers that you can use to get started. Next, you'll want to figure out how much housing will cost in the regions you plan to visit. If you are housesitting, participating in a homestay, staying with family or friends, or doing a home exchange for part or all of your trip, then your housing expenses will be less than if you are renting apartments or staying in hostels or hotels. You can estimate the costs of home rentals by going on Airbnb or VRBO websites and searching in the areas where you plan to go. If you plan to stay somewhere for more than one month, be sure to put that into your search queries as those rates will be significantly lower than the daily or weekly rates for any rental property.

Housing costs will definitely vary by location. Even small rental properties in Tokyo will be more expensive than a comfortable beach bungalow in Thailand. If most of the regions you will be visiting are on the higher end of the spectrum, then you may just need to save a bit more for your trip. The best situation is if you can balance your stays in more expensive regions (such as Paris, London, and Tokyo) with equal or greater time visiting some budget-friendly regions (such as Thailand and other places in Southeast Asia, Latin America, and Eastern Europe).

Food expenses are likely to track the cost of living in an area and will probably reflect the relative cost of housing. You can save quite a bit by eating in and cooking your own food most of the time and eating out as your budget allows. We found it to be expensive to eat out in some areas of Canada, for example, so we cooked and ate our own food most of the time we were there. On the flip side, when we were in Mexico, it seemed as though we ate out at restaurants nearly every single day since the food was utterly amazing and the prices were reasonable.

You can estimate your food costs by looking at how much on average you spend per month on food while at home. You can then take that number and plug it into an international cost of living calculator to determine how far your food budget will go in various locations around the world. Calculators can also be useful for helping you estimate local transportation, entertainment, and housing costs in a location. Check the Thank You section in the back of this book for resources that include some recommended cost of living calculators.

When you combine estimates of your big-ticket expenses with transportation, housing, and food costs, you can get a good idea of how much money you will need for your trip. You'll also need to add in any home expenses that you plan to maintain, if any. You can take the total amount and divide it by the number of trip days to get an approximate cost per day.

Create Your Savings Plan. Now it's time to make a plan for saving up the funds for your trip. If you already have a nest egg tucked away that you can use, then you may be good to go! For the rest of us, it's time to take a good hard look at our current expenses and see if there are items that we can cut back on or eliminate. Sometimes it's the little changes that can make a big difference here. For instance, do you make daily trips to Starbucks? You could save approximately $35 to $50 per week just by eliminating your daily latte. How often do you dine out during a typical week? You could stand to save a lot by cutting back and eating at home more often. These expenses can add up quickly, and if you are able to forgo some of these luxuries while preparing for your trip, your savings will grow more rapidly and you're likely be able to leave on your trip sooner.

Work While You Travel. You also might not need to save up quite as much if you plan to work while you're traveling. Maybe you can work out an arrangement with your employer to keep your current job and work while away. Or maybe you'll find some work while on your travels. With the growing digital economy, it's becoming easier to find work that you can do remotely. And while the reliability and speed of the internet can vary depending on where you go, it's rapidly getting to the point that it's possible to work from just about anywhere in the world.

My husband, Witt, was actually offered a job while we were traveling. After about eight months into our Pan Am trip our good friend, Ed, contacted Witt out of the blue to see if he was interested in a part-time position. Ed's employer needed someone to perform software tasks that no one else had the time to do. While these tasks were important for the long-term viability of the company, they were not considered to be urgent, so the tasks simply weren't getting done. They were able to work out an arrangement that suited everyone. We agreed to stay somewhere with Wi-Fi for a month or so at a stretch so Witt could do the work full-time. We could then travel full-time for several weeks and then repeat the pattern. It was fantastic. We got to spend more time in the areas that we were visiting and we were able to extend the overall length of our trip by more than one year.

However you are able to work it out, you will be glad you did. You may have to really adhere to a strict budget, or you might be able to save money with only some slight modifications to your current lifestyle. Remember that vision board that you put together in the last chapter? Take that out and really look at it. How will you feel when you are living this dream? I think you will find that the freedom you will feel is more than worth the actions you take now to bring your dream trip to life.

Stepping Boldly Forward

1. Identify your biggest expenses from your itinerary. Estimate your housing, food, entertainment, and local transportation costs for each region you plan to visit. Add these numbers up to get an estimate of your projected travel expenses. You can also divide by the total number of days of your trip to calculate your average daily budget.

2. Create a plan for reducing or eliminating your home expenses. Think about what type of situation would work best for you and decide on a strategy.

3. Develop your travel savings strategy. What actions can you take to start putting away some funds for your trip right now? What kinds of splurges can you reduce or eliminate so you can start your dream trip sooner? Look for anything that will help you to put a little extra away each month. Every little bit counts.

CHAPTER SEVEN
Making the Break

"The man who goes alone can start today: but he who travels with another must wait till that other is ready."

HENRY DAVID THOREAU

Step Five: Divulge Your Plans

Having a dream is a beautiful thing. For many of us, that's what keeps us going and makes life worth living. However, unless you take bold action upon your dreams, they simply won't happen. Simply savoring your dreams is worthwhile in itself, but without consistent action, those dreams are just ardent wishes that may never come true.

Set Your Departure Date. To transition your dream into action, you've got to set a departure date. Since you now know your rough travel itinerary, including your preferred travel seasons and chronological order for your chosen locations, you can probably narrow your departure down to an approximate time of year. You also have an estimate of how long it will take for you to save enough money for your trip. Putting this information together, you have enough to figure out your departure time to within a two to three-month period.

Now it's time to take a look at a calendar. Flip forward to the beginning of the time frame that you've determined. Look through all the calendar pages for this time period and choose a date from the mix. Maybe a big milestone like your birthday happens to fall into that time frame. You can also keep the choice simple by just selecting the first day of a month, the last day of a month, or any day in-between. Ultimately, the date can be anything that you want it to be, but you do have to settle on a single day from your calendar. Your dream doesn't become real until you set a date, so let's make it real.

Mark that date on your calendar to solidify your departure date in your mind. I find that wall calendars work best for making travel plans, since they allow you to easily visualize the time that you have to work with. It's extra helpful if your calendar also has inspiring travel photos in it. You can circle your departure with a marker, put a sticker on the day, or pin a photo of one of your destinations to that date. If appropriate, while you're at it, you can choose a date three to six months before then to purchase your departure airline tickets.

Create a Countdown Clock. Next, count how many days you have from today until the day of your departure and write that number down. Does that feel scary? It should start to feel real to you now, because the countdown to your trip departure has now officially begun! You can write that number on today's date and then count the days down as you progress through the calendar. Another method is to get a large pad of sticky notes and simply write the number of days on the top of the pad. Each day, you can pull off the top sheet and write the new number of days left on the new top page of the pad. For example, if you start your count at 250 days, then the next day, you would tear off the top sheet and write 249 days on the top page of the sticky pad. However you choose to track it, it's important to have a daily reminder that your dream is getting closer to coming true.

Post Your Inspirational Materials Prominently. Arrange your vision board, destination photos, and any other inspirational materials that you have next to your calendar and countdown pad. Put them all in a location where you are sure to see them every day (and preferably several times per day) so you have regular reminders of the amazing dream that you are actively working toward. These items will help you keep your excitement level up and your resolve strong while you prepare for your trip.

Share Your Plans Discreetly. At this point, you may be bursting at the seams to tell the whole world about your plans. Telling those closest to you is often a surefire way to share your excitement with others and to have accountability for your goals. Your personality and how confident and committed you are to your goals might all be factors in determining how you choose to proceed. I recommend that you start with telling your closest confidant and then take it from there. While telling your friends and loved ones of your plans does make it real, you also need to be careful to protect your dreams. Some people might not understand what you are doing and they might even try to talk you out of it. This is an issue that is often raised in travel circles, so it's important to at least be aware that this could also happen to you. For this reason, it's best in the early stages of preparation to share your news with those who you are confident will be supportive of your travel plans. As you build your tribe of supporters and your confidence builds, you can then branch out to others as desired.

Increase Your Perceived Value at Work. It's also a good idea to keep your plans quiet at work in the beginning, especially if your departure date is more than six months away. My good friend, Bill, told his employer about his travel plans about six months before his departure and he ended up regretting it. He stopped receiving fun work assignments because everyone else figured that he already had one foot out the door. Instead, do what you can right now to start going the extra distance at work. Put a little extra effort into each of your assignments. Help your co-workers out with their responsibilities when you can with a cheerful smile. Be the kind of colleague that you yourself would enjoy working with. The goal is to be valued as much as possible by your employer as well as your coworkers in the months leading up to the time when you do break the news of your departure. Your bargaining position will be greatly improved and you may be pleasantly surprised with the results.

Make Your Departure Plan. My husband, Witt, and I only gave our employer one month notice of our departure when we were preparing for our career break to travel through Africa. We both worked for the same employer at the time and we had researched our company's leave policy. The policy, as written, only allowed for up to three months off for personal reasons and we knew that wouldn't be enough time for us to do the trip as we had planned it. We were committed to our trip and had decided that we were going to do it even if we had to quit our jobs, but we hoped for the best anyway.

We each gave our notice to our respective managers and what happened next blew us away. Our managers collaborated with our company's human resources department and together they figured out a way to give us more than one year of leave from work. We couldn't believe it! Not only could we do our trip as we'd planned it, but we would also be welcomed back into comparable positions in the company when we returned.

Maintain Good Relations with Your Employer. Regardless of your circumstances, it is important to exit work gracefully. You want to keep your future employment options as bright as possible. You may decide to return to work at your current employer, but you might not. Either way, leaving for your trip while on good terms with your employer can only help you later. Depending upon your situation, you might consider asking for letters of recommendation from your employer while you are still working there. This is also a good time to polish up your resumé in case you find a great opportunity while you are traveling.

We didn't even bother to ask for leave from our employers when we were preparing for our career break for our Pan Am trip. We were planning to be away much longer this time and we didn't feel right about asking for leave when we knew that we'd likely be away for at least one to one and a half years. In addition, I knew at the time that I was ready for a significant career change and making a clean break just seemed to make the most sense. Witt ultimately decided to do the same even though he loved his job and might've been happy returning there after his trip.

We'd learned from our earlier experiences that our priorities could significantly change while traveling. We knew that we had no way to know what we would want to do when (or if) we returned. So we decided to give ourselves more freedom this time around so we could follow our hearts wherever they led us.

It was definitely a riskier decision but we are really glad that we did it. When we returned from our travels, we were able to move to a new town and establish a different kind of lifestyle for ourselves. We wouldn't have been able to do that as easily if we'd still felt tethered to our previous jobs. We made sure to save up a bit more money to help with our re-entry and so we would have an extra cushion to use while we got our bearings.

You can size up your situation now to consider what you might want to do. There really is no wrong answer, but you do need to have faith in yourself and your abilities. Trust in your capabilities. Know that you will figure it all out when it's time to do so.

Stepping Boldly Forward

1. Set your departure date and create your countdown clock. Keep inspirational reminders of your travel plans displayed prominently so you can keep your excitement level high as you prepare for your departure.

2. Begin to build your support team now. Identify close friends and family members who will rally behind you and keep you moving toward your goals. Join travel forums and Facebook groups to get additional support and inspiration from other travelers.

3. Do a little digging to see whether your company has a leave policy that you can use to take time off for your trip. Sabbaticals are common practice in some professions, so investigate to see if that's an option for you. Know how much time you will need for your trip so you can best decide upon your plan of action.

4. Find out if you can take your job with you. Consider putting together a proposal which explains how you plan to schedule your work and maintain open communications with your employer while traveling.

CHAPTER EIGHT
Unplugging Your Life

"The journey of a thousand miles begins with one step."

LAO TZU

Step Six: Run Your Life Remotely

While you are out in the world enjoying your travels, you will still need a way to manage whatever home affairs you leave behind. This involves creating some kind of plan to take care of your home, your personal belongings, your correspondence, and your bills while you're away. It's worthwhile to put considerable effort into these preparations now so that you don't have to worry about it while you are traveling.

Minimize Your Home Expenses. One task that you can begin even in the earliest stages of the planning process is eliminating unnecessary expenses. As I mentioned previously, getting rid of your home expenses allows you to save money faster so you can depart on your trip sooner, travel longer, splurge more often while traveling, and generally be more comfortable financially. Start out by eliminating any memberships or subscriptions that you rarely use. Review your credit card statements to identify any recurring expenses that you could live without. Make a plan for every recurring item that you find. Your goal is to get the charges down to zero by your departure date.

Sift Through Your Stuff. Reducing your personal belongings down to the items that you truly value will make your life simpler logistically. It'll be easier to pack up and go and it'll be much easier when you return if you don't have as much stuff to deal with. In addition, you will be surprised to find how wonderfully freeing it feels to clean out the cobwebs and lighten your load.

As consumers, we tend to be great at accumulating stuff. We buy clothes, gadgets, cars, furniture, and all sorts of knickknacks to fill our homes and our lives. Few of us are able to find time to deal with the amount of stuff that we have. Even if we may not find something useful anymore, we can often find a spot to store it in a closet, our basement, or our garage.

This happens to all of us to some degree. Witt and I sometimes joke that it doesn't matter how much space we have to work with, we end up filling it with stuff.

The problem is that it takes real energy to deal with our stuff. We buy stuff to fill some need in our lives, so we tell ourselves that we *need* our stuff. We believe that our stuff is there to serve us, when really we are the ones who end up serving our stuff. We trip over it in our entryways. We can feel the energy drain out of us any time we have to deal with our cluttered closet or when we're trying to find something stored away in a crowded garage or basement.

We may be able to tolerate the clutter and these energy drains for quite a while, until we have to move our stuff. Just the thought of doing a house move is enough to convince some people to stay put ... where they are ... forever.

This is where you get to put on your big girl pants and take responsibility for all the stuff in your life. Acknowledge to yourself that you have more stuff in your life than you probably really need to have. Then commit to making the time to go through everything you have. If you have a garage, I recommend that you start there. Perhaps you can move your car to your driveway so you can use the space in your garage as a staging area.

You'll want to make several piles with your stuff. There will be the stuff you keep and the stuff you don't. For the latter group, you can sell it, donate it, or give it away to someone you know who can use it. Selling your stuff is great because you can apply the proceeds to your travel fund. You may also get a tax write-off for any donations that you make. For some items that are difficult to part with, it can feel good to find a friend or family member who would really appreciate it and give it to them. If possible, it's best to reduce your belongings down to your keepsakes and valuable items that cannot be easily replaced.

The challenge can be in figuring out which items go into which pile. In Marie Kondo's book, *The Life-Changing Magic of Tidying Up*, she suggests that you hold each item in your hands to determine whether the item brings you joy. If the answer is an immediate yes, then keep it. If you hesitate at all, then choose another pile to put it in. Whenever you get overwhelmed, remind yourself that you are taking care of your stuff now so you won't have to do it later. Take breaks if you need to, but don't give up. Every box that you keep is something that you will have to store and move later. If it's not worth your energy to deal with it now, then when will it be worth your energy? And if it's not worth your energy at all, then why do you have it? Take care of it now, so you (or your loved ones) don't have to deal with it later. The freedom that you feel when you reduce your belongings down to those that you most want is worth it. Remember that everything you keep will have to be stored while you're away. Commercial storage space fees can add up over the length of your trip, so it is worth it to aim for the smallest storage space that you can get away with.

I used to have an extensive book collection. As an avid reader, I am continually buying new books to read. These days I mostly buy electronic books, but there was a time when I had bookcases and boxes of books that I moved with me whenever I changed households. In one of our early downsizing exercises, Witt asked me if we could get rid of my college textbooks. I wanted to keep them as they were a reminder to me of how hard I worked in college. I loved displaying them in my office at work because they exemplified the knowledge that I'd learned and I felt a certain amount of prestige in displaying them.

Witt asked me when the last time was that I opened one of these books. The truth was that I hadn't opened a single one in years, and I didn't even feel the need to do so then. To my horror, he suggested that we sell them. He promised me that if I ever had the need for the information in one of the books, we could replace them. I reluctantly agreed.

But you know what? The hardest part for me was in actually making the decision. Once the books were gone, I didn't miss them one bit. I haven't even once felt the need to hold them in my hands or replace them. We were able to earn more than $1000 with the sale of those books, which of course went directly into our travel fund. But the best part for me, by far, is that I never had to move or store those heavy books again.

Make a Plan for Your Home. While you are in the process of downsizing your stuff, it's a good idea to start thinking about what to do with your home while you're away. If you're renting your home, then all you'll likely need to do is notify your landlord in advance of breaking your lease, put your stuff into storage, pack your bags, and go. If you own your home, you'll want to think about whether it makes more sense for you to rent your place out while you're away or to sell it. There are advantages and disadvantages to both approaches, and it really comes down to personal preference. Do you know for sure that you'll want to move back into your current home? Or would you rather have the opportunity to move somewhere new—even if you decide to move back to the same town?

You'll also want to factor in whether your spouse will be traveling with you or staying behind at home. Sometimes it may not be possible or practical for both of you to travel. If he'll be staying at home, then you may not have to make as many decisions about your current home. If he'll be traveling with you, he can assist with the preparations so you can get it done more efficiently.

Depending on the economy and where you live, renting your home out may be easier than selling it. We've rented our homes out for our trips and we found it to be super easy. One time we found a couple through some good friends who needed a place to stay for a year. They took good care of our place and always paid on time. When we returned, we decided to move to another part of town so we then sold our townhome. Another time, we hired a property manager to rent our place out and they promptly found some great tenants for us. Even though we decided to move to another part of the state when we returned, those same reliable tenants have been renting from us ever since we departed on our trip.

Managing Correspondence and Paying the Bills. You'll also need to decide how you want to manage your remaining responsibilities while you're away. You can ask someone to take care of them for you ... or you can do it all yourself. What you'll need is someone to handle your mail and pay your bills for you while you're traveling. If you want a trusted relative or friend to take care of your mail for you, it'll involve them opening your mail and having access to your finances to pay whatever home bills you still have while you are traveling. We asked Witt's parents to handle this for us on one of our trips. They were happy to do that for us and they did a fantastic job, but we still felt at times that it was a big imposition.

These days, there are services that can handle your mail for you. You forward your mail to them via your own personal mailbox address and, for a small monthly fee, they scan the outside of all of your mail for you. You log into your online account to see the scans, decide which ones you'd like them to open for you and then discard the rest. They will scan the contents of the mail that you request so you can read your mail online, save the PDF for future reference, and forward the physical mail to someone to handle for you if desired.

Minimize the Mountain of Paper. In both cases, you'll still want to do what you can reduce the amount of physical mail that you regularly receive. It's now possible to elect to receive your credit card statements, bank statements, and many other forms of business correspondence by email instead of in paper form. This is easiest because you can deal with these yourself from wherever you have access to your email account. Cancel any remaining subscriptions or memberships that you have to further reduce the physical mail that gets sent to you. You can also take action to get yourself off of any mailing lists that you are on to eliminate junk mail. Once you have taken each of these steps, your physical mail can be reduced down to only a few items per month. This will make managing your home life much easier to deal with while you are away, and you can then just have your mail forwarded to your trusted friend's address or to your virtual mailbox service address.

Create a Virtual Filing Cabinet. It'll also be helpful to have a way to file copies of your bills, important documents, and other items electronically so you can easily have access to them wherever you are in the world. I especially like to use Dropbox for this, because you can store all your important papers and have access to them even when you are offline. You could also experiment with other software platforms, such as Evernote and Google Drive, for this purpose. What you'll want is a secure place where you can store electronic copies of important papers such as your birth certificates, marriage license, the front pages of your passport, prescriptions, and proof of medical insurance. You can also use the software you choose as a virtual filing cabinet for any correspondence that you need to keep on hand.

Get Your Passport Ready. Of course, you'll also need to make arrangements for your travel papers. If you don't already have a passport, you'll want to get one right away. If you do have one, then you'll need to take a closer look at the expiration date of your passport. You'll want to have enough time to complete your travels plus still have at least an additional six months left before your passport expires. If this is not the case, make the time now to apply for a new passport. Depending upon your travel plans, you might even consider applying for a passport that comes with extra pages.

Plan for Obtaining Visas. If there are any countries that you plan to visit that will not provide visas to you upon entry, you'll need to plan ahead for that too. This could possibly involve sending your passport away to a foreign embassy that has offices in your home country. Often though, you can get visas while you are traveling by visiting an embassy or consulate in a neighboring country to the one you want to visit. For example, while we were in Gabon, we visited embassies for the Congo, the Democratic Republic of Congo, and Angola, and we were able to get visas within 24 hours for each country. Sometimes the process only takes a few hours, but we've had it happen where we've had to leave our visa applications and our passports at the embassy overnight. Everything was done professionally and all turned out fine, but it's understandable if you would rather not have that experience. For best results, I recommend that you arrive at the embassy or consulate early in the day so you can leave the same day with both your passport and your new visa.

You now have the tools and resources in place to run your life remotely. You've simplified your life by reducing the stuff you have and the mail you receive down to a manageable size. You also now have a passport with enough time left on it for you to complete your trip, you've given some thought into what kind of visas you will need, and you have a rough plan for how you will obtain them. You can now travel confidently knowing that everything at home has been taken care of properly. Most importantly, you have given yourself the ultimate gift: the gift of freedom.

Stepping Boldly Forward

1. Take a good look at the items that you've got laying around your home, including in your closets, your garage, your attic, and your basement. Set aside several weekends for the purpose of going through all of your things, one box at a time. Use this opportunity to really take charge of the stuff that you carry around in your life.

2. Decide what you want to do with your home while you're away. If you want to sell your home, be sure to give yourself enough time to get through the whole process before you depart. If you're going to rent your home, decide how you want to do that.

3. Create an online filing cabinet and store copies of all of your important documents in there.

4. Check your passport expiration date. Be sure to give yourself enough time to complete your trip with six months to spare. Apply for a new one if necessary.

5. Investigate the visa requirements of each country on your itinerary. Determine now whether you need to apply for a visa before you depart or if you will be able to visit a consulate or embassy for that country while you are traveling.

CHAPTER NINE
Staying Healthy

"An inconvenience is only an adventure wrongly considered; an adventure is an inconvenience rightly considered."

GILBERT KEITH CHESTERTON

Step Seven: Ensure Your Health

One concern that you might have when you consider traveling abroad is your health. How do you stay healthy while away from home? And what happens if you do get sick? What do you do and where do you go?

The Odds Are on Your Side. Health care is generally excellent and affordable in many places in the world. In fact, in many parts of the world, you can walk into a doctor's office or medical clinic and receive stellar treatment for little to no cost. Even in relatively poor countries, it is usually possible to access quality healthcare in larger cities. Please allow me to share a personal story with you to illustrate this point.

My husband's parents, Henry and Kathy, came to visit us a few years ago when we were in Cuenca, Ecuador, over the Christmas holidays. An all-day Christmas parade is the tradition in Cuenca and people from villages throughout Ecuador had traveled there to participate. While we were outside watching this parade, Kathy tripped on some uneven concrete and did a face plant onto the sidewalk. The result was a large gash over her right eyebrow. Paramedic teams were already on the scene because of the large crowds present. As soon as they saw Kathy's injury, they rushed over to us and began treating her wound.

Witt and I translated the conversation as the paramedics asked questions about how she was injured and collected other relevant health history information. The gash over Kathy's eye was fairly deep, so the paramedics offered to take Kathy to the hospital so she could get some stitches. An ambulance was nearby so Witt accompanied his mom and the paramedics to a nearby hospital where she was promptly treated. After the stitches were neatly in place, Witt and Kathy asked the medical staff where they could pay for the services she'd received. Surprisingly, no payment was required. The paramedics even offered them a ride back to the parade in the ambulance!

A few days later, Kathy needed to get her stitches removed, so Kathy and Henry jumped into a taxi and asked the driver to take them to the nearest hospital. As before, Kathy received immediate treatment. This time, though, the medical staff made a point of telling them emphatically that it would cost five (US) dollars to remove the stitches and asked if that would be ok with them. Henry and Kathy gladly consented so the staff promptly removed the stitches. Afterward, Henry and Kathy thanked the friendly medical staff and paid the $5. Then they walked out the front door of the hospital and climbed into a taxi. There was no paperwork to fill out and the whole experience was quick and easy.

We've had similar positive experiences with medical care we received in other countries. For example, when we required medical treatment in Guatemala and Chile, we simply walked into a rural clinic and promptly received the care that we needed. When Witt had a stomach bug in Peru, a doctor made a house-call to our apartment to provide wonderful in-person care. In each of these cases, we paid the equivalent of less than US $40 for prompt, professional treatment.

We also visited several dental offices during our travels for preventative care. We've had our teeth cleaned professionally in South Africa, Mexico, Ecuador, and Chile. In Mexico, we even found a wonderful pediatric dentist who cleaned Quinn's teeth while still managing to make him comfortable in the dentist chair.

This dentist also took quite a bit of time to explain to us that Quinn was going to need orthodontics fairly soon. Even though our Spanish skills were a little rough the dentist was very patient with us to be sure that we understood him. In all, he spent about three hours talking with us and answering our questions. We were grateful and impressed with the level of service that he gave to us.

Purchase a Travel Health Insurance Policy. Since accidents can happen anywhere that you are, I believe it's important to be prepared. Purchasing a travel health insurance policy can provide you with an extra safety net and some valuable peace of mind. Even though excellent medical care is widely available, it's a good idea to have a policy that covers you in the event something unfortunate does happen.

Think about the kinds of places you plan to go and the types of activities you plan to participate in. For example, do you plan to hike in the Himalayas? What if you twist your ankle somewhere on the trail? While you can undoubtedly get a ride out on the back of a yak, I believe in also having a backup plan.

Travel health insurance premiums are often much more affordable than those for your home health insurance policy. The main feature you'll want to look for is a policy that covers evacuation and repatriation back to your home country. As with other forms of insurance, this is definitely one of those situations where you hope that you never have to use it, but you'll be really glad to have it if you do.

We've had good experiences with the insurance offered through World Nomads. It cost us about $2400 per year for a policy to cover our family of three. This policy covered everything that we needed it to cover, including "riskier" activities that we enjoy like scuba diving and mountain biking. While we were traveling, we submitted several claims with them and they were all promptly paid in full.

There are several other companies that offer travel health insurance, so it's worth it to shop around. Be sure to read the fine print so you have a clear idea of what is covered and what is not. The cost of the premiums and the level of coverage will likely vary depending upon your home country as well as the countries that you plan to visit.

Some policies will also cover the loss or damage to your valuables, such as electronics, as long as you can prove how much you paid for the items. Be sure that you have copies of all your receipts from your electronics saved away and accessible via your online filing cabinet. If your items are lost or stolen, you might also need to file a report with the local police to prove your claim.

Visit a Travel Medical Clinic. At least a few months before you depart, I also recommend that you visit a medical clinic that specializes in foreign travel. These clinics are staffed with doctors and nurses who are well-versed in international travel and they can give you informed advice about how to stay healthy while on your trip.

If possible, be able to tell them specifically where you plan to go, when you plan to be there, and approximately how long you plan to stay in each region. They will be able to tell you what vaccinations they recommend for you and you can often receive them during your office visit. The travel doctors can also give you prescriptions for powerful antibiotics in the event that you get sick while abroad and they can advise you on whether it's better to fill the prescriptions before you depart or once you are in a specific country on your itinerary.

Sometimes it may be necessary to space your vaccinations out by a month or more when receiving them in a series, so you'll want to be sure that you have enough time prior to your departure to get all the shots that you need. For example, the vaccination to prevent Hepatitis B is often administered as a series of three shots given over a six-month period of time. Also, some countries require proof of certain vaccinations prior to entry. For example, proof of yellow fever vaccinations is often required for entry into countries located near the Amazon Basin. In other cases, vaccinations may be optional, so it's purely your choice as to whether you want to take the recommended precautions.

Fill Your Current Prescriptions. If you have any ongoing health concerns, you'll want to get your prescriptions for your medications filled before you depart. It may be worth asking your doctor for extra copies of your prescriptions in case you need them while you are traveling. Depending upon where you are going and what type of medication you require, you may be able to buy what you need at a pharmacy without even needing a written prescription. It also might be much less expensive to purchase your medication while you are traveling than while you are in your home country. You can ask for advice during your visit at the travel clinic. The travel doctor may have specific knowledge that will help you make informed decisions. If they don't know for sure at the clinic, then it's best to fill up your prescriptions before you depart.

Take Along a First-Aid Kit. You might also consider packing a small first-aid kit to take with you. Even if you plan to stay in areas that have easy access to modern health facilities, it's a good idea to put together a small medical kit. You could include items such as headache medication, Band-Aids, allergy medication, and medication to treat intestinal issues. These are all items that you can buy and replenish as you go, but it's nice to have them handy in case you find yourself needing them while on a long flight or bus ride.

If you do plan to venture into the wilderness or go to places more remote from modern facilities, you might consider bringing along your own bandages and sterilized syringes in case you need them. You can always donate them to a local medical clinic if you don't end up using them.

Brush Up on Your First-Aid Skills. Whenever we are preparing to travel into remote regions for significant periods of time, we like to take a Wilderness First Aid course before we depart. The National Outdoor Leadership School (NOLS) offers a wonderful three-day course where you can learn how to handle various situations when medical help may not be readily available. As a mom, and a former Girl Scout, it gives me peace of mind to know that I would know what to do in some of the more common medical situations.

Prioritize Sanitation. Often the best way to stay healthy, wherever you are, is by making sanitation a priority. Wash your hands frequently with soap and clean water. Be sure that your drinking water is safe and filtered. Wash your produce thoroughly before eating. A great practice is to soak fresh fruits and vegetables in a bowl filled with clean water and a few drops of grapefruit seed extract. A tiny bottle goes a long way and it's easy to toss into your purse or travel bag so you always have it with you.

Flock to Dinner. When eating out at restaurants, opt to dine in a place with high turnover instead of a place with empty tables. This helps to ensure that the food you are served is likely to be fresh. Appearances can be deceiving as simple family-owned restaurants are sometimes safer than swankier establishments. I like to look for restaurants that are filled with local clients instead of only tourists. Locals are more likely to be repeat or regular customers at restaurants, so that's a good indication that the food is safe and delicious.

It's also usually fine to eat street food. This is a great way to sample local dishes wherever you are, and I highly recommend it. With street vendors, you can often watch as your food is prepared so you know what you are getting. If a food cart has a line of locals in front of it, the chances are good that you've hit the street food jackpot. Get yourself in line and prepare yourself for a wonderful and authentic culinary treat.

Now you have a number of tools, tips, and resources at your disposal so you can stay healthy while traveling. Everyone has a different style and comfort zone, so feel free to use what you find helpful so you can implement these practices when you need them.

Stepping Boldly Forward

1. Investigate the travel health insurance options available to you. Read the small print to confirm that you will be covered everywhere you plan to go and for all the activities that you plan to participate in.

2. Put together a small medical kit to take with you. Include some basic medical supplies as well as your own prescription medications.

3. If you will be spending significant amounts time in remote villages, consider packing extra supplies and taking a wilderness first aid course.

4. Make sanitation a priority. Keep your hands clean, drink filtered water, and wash your fresh produce before eating. Select your restaurants and food carts based upon the number of locals that frequent there.

CHAPTER TEN
What to Pack

"When preparing to travel, lay out all your clothes and all your money. Then take half the clothes and twice the money."

SUSAN HELLER

Step Eight: Assemble Your Kit

We seldom use everything that we pack when going on a trip. This tends to be even more true when we are packing to go on a longer adventure. Our minds often go into overdrive trying to think of everything that we might possibly need on our trip and we worry about forgetting something important. The unfortunate result is that our luggage ends up being far too heavy to carry around even for a very short time. Some travelers find later that they have to ditch items because of weight issues or because they discover that they didn't actually need many of the items that they'd originally packed.

Pack Light. It really is worth the effort to attempt to travel light because it gives you the freedom to move around more easily. The good news is that you can probably buy all that you need along the way. There are stores, shops, and markets everywhere in the world. If you find that you really need something, the chances are very good that you can find it regardless of where you happen to be. You will also find that buying as you go about your trip is a great way to get clothes appropriate for the local climate as well as to pick up some wearable souvenirs from your travels.

There can be some exceptions to this. If you wear a larger-than-average shoe size, for example, then you may have difficulty in some parts of the world finding shoes in your size. If this is the case for you, it will be especially important that you pack what you need before you depart.

Put Your Best Foot Forward. So let's start by putting some serious thought into what kinds of shoes to bring with you. Since we're aiming to pack light, I recommend that you bring no more than two or three pairs of shoes in total. Anything more than that will take up too much space in your bag and be a nuisance to carry around. When choosing which shoes to bring with you, the number one requirement is that your shoes must be comfortable to wear.

When you are traveling, you are likely to spend much more time walking than you do at home. You'll be walking through airports and train stations and browsing through outdoor markets and museums. You'll also find yourself walking around while exploring each town that you visit. Your shoes need to be comfortable enough to wear all day long and sturdy enough to hold up to months of daily walking. If your shoes are not comfortable, you'll find that you simply will not wear them and if they are not sturdy and well-made, they won't last long on your trip. Splurging a little on some good quality shoes will likely be worth the investment so you can have a wonderful and comfortable trip.

You'll also want to be able to wear your shoes in all sorts of weather conditions if possible. If you'll mainly be in warmer climates then a pair of well-made sandals may be just what you need. Even so, you'll also likely want to have a pair of regular shoes for times when sandals are neither practical nor appropriate. In all cases, do what you can to ensure that your shoes will be able to stand up to walking in puddles or pouring rain.

Since you will be wearing the same shoes nearly every day, it is important that you genuinely like your shoes and want to be seen in them. With all the other requirements that we just discussed this may seem like a tall order, but there are many shoe options available these days and some are marketed specifically for travelers. You can shop around until you find the right pair of shoes for you.

You might also want to have a dressier shoe option for special occasions or for going out somewhere fancy. Women can often pack a pair of ballet flats or Mary-Jane style shoes for this purpose as they are easy to pack and don't take up much space. Men can usually just get away with a dark pair of shoes or sneakers that are in reasonably good condition.

Hand-Washable Socks and Undergarments. The socks that you wear are just as important as your shoes. If you tend to have clammy feet like I do, wearing good quality socks can make a huge difference in your comfort level. Your feet will have fewer blisters even in hot weather and your feet will be warmer in cold weather. I recommend staying away from cotton whenever possible. Instead choose a brand like Thörlo or SmartWool that will dry quickly and be durable enough to go the distance for you. You can even rinse or wash your socks at nighttime in a bathroom sink, wring them out, and hang them up so they'll be ready for you to wear again when you wake up in the morning. Choose the sock thickness appropriate to the climate where you will be.

Similarly, when choosing your undergarments, opt for synthetic fabrics that will dry quickly in any situation. I like ExOfficio brand because I can wash them in the evening and hang them overnight and have a clean pair ready to go for when I need them. If you know you will be visiting colder climates, you can also bring a set of long underwear with you to give you some added warmth. As a bonus, they can also double as a warm pair of pajamas when needed.

Mixing and Matching is Key. When it comes to choosing clothes to bring on your trip, you'll want to use the same practical kind of lens. No matter what your style, you want to choose versatile and comfortable pieces that can be worn over and over again in a variety of situations.

Every garment that you bring should ideally be machine-washable and easy-to-care-for. You'll also want the option to add layers to be comfortable in cooler weather, so it's best if your clothes are in neutral tones or in one color palette so you can mix and match your pieces together.

I recommend bringing about three to four changes of clothes along with a selection of colorful accessories and add-ons so you can alter your look for any occasion. Many women travelers love to bring along a sarong or a large scarf because it can be used as a skirt, a shawl, or even as a blanket when traveling. In general, the more versatile your garments are, the happier you will be.

Consider Local Customs. You'll also want to consider the customs at your destinations when deciding which clothes to bring. In some places there are strict rules and in other places choosing to adhere to the dress code is merely a sign of respect for the local culture. For example, it's usually required that legs be covered when visiting Buddhist temples so you'd want to bring along a pair of pants or a long skirt if that's in your plans. Also, while the dress code might not explicitly apply to those visiting Muslim countries, you're less likely to draw unwanted attention to yourself if you make a reasonable effort to cover up your arms, legs, and head.

Climate Preparations. A good waterproof jacket with a hood is a very practical option to bring along as it can provide great protection against heavy rain, wind, and cooler weather. If it's easily packable, you can stow it in your day pack for walking around town and know that you'll be prepared if the weather takes an unexpected turn. An insulating layer like a fleece pullover or sweater can be added underneath to increase your comfort on cooler days. If you plan to be traveling in colder areas, you might consider investing in a packable down jacket. Many manufacturers today offer down jackets that can be folded down to a very small size. When the jacket is packed into its pouch, it can double as a pillow that you can use on long flights or other transportation legs. A knit hat and a pair of gloves are easy to pack and can make a huge difference in your comfort in a wide range of situations. You might also want to bring a hat with a brim to protect you on sunny days. There are types of sun-hats available that fold well for traveling and are easy to pull out when you need them.

Back to Basics. When it comes to packing toiletries, less is definitely more. Toiletries can be heavy to carry, so you might want to rethink bringing along your entire collection of products to support an elaborate beauty routine. As much as you can, keep it simple. When you are on the move, you can pack enough toiletries to last for a few weeks and then replenish as you go. This is a great opportunity for you to try new brands and to use fewer products than you do at home.

Bringing Your Phone. You might also want to bring along your cell or mobile phone as it's like having a computer at your fingertips. Your phone is also a great option for taking photos to document your trip. Even if you plan to bring a camera along, your phone can serve as an easy-to-access-and-use back-up camera.

You can choose to extend your current data plan so you can have coverage wherever you go, but this can be an expensive option for a longer trip. Another alternative is to purchase a SIM card for your unlocked phone in each country that you visit. SIM cards are usually only about $1 to $2 to purchase and they give your phone a local number so that it's easier to make phone calls within that country. You can purchase a pre-paid data plan for about $20 so you can also have web access even when you're away from wifi.

There are numerous ways to keep in touch with loved ones while you're traveling. The least expensive and easiest options involve using wifi whenever it is available. Common communication methods include email, texting using WhatsApp or Facebook Messenger, or video calls using Skype, FaceTime, or Facebook Messenger.

Communications and Other Electronics. To aid with these kinds of communications, you might consider bringing along your laptop, tablet, or e-book reader. The type of device that you choose to bring is completely up to you, but you'll definitely want to give some serious consideration to factors like weight and convenience. Bringing a laptop makes sense if you intend to work while traveling, but it's definitely larger and heavier than most tablets and e-book readers. Tablets are more portable but can also be less practical to use for longer work sessions. E-book readers are great for bringing large numbers of books and guidebooks with you without weighing down your luggage. Whatever you choose to bring, be sure to pack charge cords and whatever other accessories that you need. While you're at it, you might also need to pack an outlet converter so you can plug in your devices when you are visiting the countries on your itinerary.

Accessing Your Money. You'll want to bring along a selection of credit cards and debit cards. Be sure to check the expiration dates on your cards to determine whether you'll need a replacement while you are traveling. You'll also want to notify your bank and credit card companies of your travel schedule so that you don't get locked out of being able to use your cards. Keep all of your card pins and passwords stored in eWallet or another secure password app for safe keeping and easy lookup.

I like to use bank accounts that have minimal foreign transaction fees and ATM charges. Companies like Charles Schwab and Fidelity offer debit cards without any transaction fees and are super easy to obtain if you already happen to have investment accounts with them. Contact your current bank to find out what kinds of fees they charge for international transactions. Consider that even small fees can add up over time, so you may want to look into opening up one or more additional accounts so you have increased options to use while traveling.

Not all debit cards and credit cards are accepted everywhere so it's a good idea to have multiple options available to you. Getting cash from an ATM is by far the best and easiest way to obtain cash in local currencies in most places. However, it is worth it to take some reasonable precautions to protect your travel funds. You might have debit cards to bank accounts that are only used for travel, for example, and only use those while overseas. You can keep smaller balances in these accounts and replenish the funds as needed via electronic transfer.

Just like you might do at home, use some common sense when selecting an ATM to withdraw your money. If it's at all possible, choose to use ATMs that offer higher levels of security. For example, it's better to use the ATMs inside of bank buildings than those in public places. Withdraw only what you need for the next few days. If you plan to carry larger amounts, divvy up your cash to stash it in two to three different places so you are sure to always have some cash with you. A money belt can come in handy for keeping your large bills as well as back-up ATM and credit cards with you at all times.

License to Drive. If you plan to do any driving on your trip, you'll want to make sure that your driver's license won't expire while you're traveling. You can also apply for an international driver's license to make it easier to rent a car or a scooter if desired.

You now have some practical tips and ideas about what kinds of personal items to bring with you. Keeping your packing list on the smaller side will help you tremendously not only when it comes to carrying your luggage around with you, but also in keeping track of your things while you are on the move. The less that you have with you, the easier it will be for you overall and the more freedom you will feel.

Stepping Boldly Forward

1. Review your itinerary and determine the kind of weather and temperatures you are likely to encounter while traveling.

2. Settle on how many pairs of shoes that you want to bring with you. Explore some possibilities outside of your usual footwear selection to see if you can find options that will work for you in a wide variety of situations. Try the shoes on and walk around in them to ensure proper fit and comfort.

3. Choose your clothes to provide the maximum versatility for a wide variety of situations. Consider it a welcome challenge to find just the right combination of garments to have for the kinds of environments that you will be experiencing.

4. Keep your toiletry list to a minimum. Decide now what you absolutely need to take with you. Challenge your choices and see if you still stand by them.

5. Think about what kinds of gadgets you want to bring with you such as a laptop, tablet, e-reader, phone, or camera. Be sure to bring charge cords and needed accessories for each one.

6. Review your credit and debit card options to determine what you will take with you.

CHAPTER ELEVEN
Overcoming Roadblocks

*"You lose sight of things... and when
you travel, everything balances out."*

DARANNA GIDEL

Step Nine: Conquer Your Obstacles

E ven after following this process, there are bound
to be obstacles that will come up for you. One of
the most common issues that can occur is when
friends or family don't want you to go. This can
be very difficult to deal with, can cause all sorts of self-
doubt, and you might even reconsider whether you are
making the right decision.

First of all, if you've read this far in this book, then you
are making the right decision for you. You simply would
not have picked up this book and read it if your heart wasn't

pulling you in this direction. Something inside of you knows deep down that you want to take a break to travel and part of you probably desperately needs it too.

Remember Your Why. It's time to do some serious soul-searching. Look ahead to what your life might be like in 5, 10, or 15 years. What happens to you and the rest of your life if you don't take your dream trip? What parts of you will diminish if you don't do this? Will you look back on this decision point in a few years and see it as a missed opportunity? What other dreams will you also forgo? Most people find that, when they reflect back on their younger years, they tend to regret what they didn't do more than what they actually did. Don't let this opportunity pass you by. Be the person you've always wanted to be.

Look Beyond the Comments. There are many reasons why your friends and family might not want you to go, and most of them may not have anything to do with you. First of all, people have a tendency to project their own insecurities onto you. It's human nature and unfortunately, it can be a fairly common occurrence with those closest to us. Many times, when others have given up on their own dreams in the past, they have difficulty supporting you while you are so obviously following your dreams. The people who will be most supportive to you are those who have also acted boldly in their own lives to follow their dreams. You will likely find out which of your loved ones is in each group soon after announcing your plans, if you don't already know. Love them all anyway. Stay close to the dream followers as they are your cheering squad and your best source of moral support.

Share What You've Learned. Another reason that your friends and family might not want you to take your trip is they are genuinely concerned for your safety. This is where your detailed preparations for your trip, your newfound knowledge of the specific places you are going, and the on-the-ground information that you've learned from other travelers becomes invaluable. Armed with reliable, detailed information, you can more easily share what you know to put your loved ones at ease. Nothing works better to calm down vague fears than relaying first-hand accounts of other travelers' wonderful experiences in the specific places that you plan to visit.

Your friends and family also don't want to lose the "you" that they have come to know and appreciate. They love you as you are now – the person who goes out to coffee with them, shares the same jokes, and goes to the same gym. They may worry that you might not ever come back from your travels, or that when you do come back, you'll be a different person than you are now. You can take solace in the knowledge that by being true to your dreams, you are actually becoming more aligned with the real you. You are stripping away any façade that has developed over time, and the person who you are deep down inside is now ready to live the life that you were always meant to live.

Keep in Touch. Create and share your plan to keep in touch with those closest to you while you're away. This will help your friends and family through the transition of letting you go and give them some peace of mind that they will still have you in their lives. You can offer to make regular video calls with those closest to you so your loved ones can sleep better at night. There's something incredibly soothing about hearing your voice, seeing your smiling face, and listening to the details of your adventures that does wonders for those who are most concerned about your well-being. Your family and friends will get to live vicariously through you and they'll be relieved to know that you care enough about them to make reaching out to them a priority in your life.

You can also set up a blog to keep friends and family up to date with your latest adventures. While it can get cumbersome writing detailed letters or emails to several different people during your trip, it's far easier to share your stories and photos with others via your website so that even distant acquaintances can follow along with your travels. You might be surprised to discover that people who you hardly knew before are regularly reading about your adventures while sipping their morning coffee and looking for some inspiration for themselves. Your blog also serves as a great memento of your trip that you can fondly look back upon and share with others long after you return.

Battling Your Own Fears. You might also find yourself running up against your own fears from time to time. This is a completely normal part of getting out of your comfort zone, so, every once in a while, you're gonna find yourself getting cold feet. Whenever that happens, remind yourself why it's important for you to break free from your current life. Look at the beautiful photos on your vision board so you can recapture the feelings of excitement that you had when you first created it. Search for travel blogs to follow so you can maintain your motivation and so you can keep your own excitement and inspiration elevated. Join travel-themed Facebook groups so you can ask questions and look for advice and inspiration from other travelers.

When it all comes down to it, you simply have to take the leap and trust that it will all work out. Follow your heart and allow the details to take care of themselves.

Stepping Boldly Forward

1. Identify your strongest supporters and align yourself with them.

2. Settle on a plan on how and when to break the news to everyone else, including those who might be less enthusiastic about your upcoming departure.

3. Be prepared to answer their questions and tell them why it is important that you take this trip. Sharing stories from others who have traveled to these regions can also help.

4. Develop a plan to stay in communication with your friends and family.

5. Remind yourself frequently why this trip is important to you. Follow your heart and trust that it will all work out.

CONCLUSION
My Wish For You

*"Life is not measured by the number of breaths we take,
but by the moments that take our breath away."*

VICKI CORONA

Step Ten: Hit the Road

Congratulations! You did it! You have conquered your fears, taken the leap of faith, and embraced your dreams. You have boldly stepped out of your comfort zone and into your growth zone. Now it is time to embark on your dream adventure and feel the freedom that is waiting for you.

As part of our journey together thus far, you have come to the realization that you both want and need to take a break from the rat race so you can travel slowly and deliberately. You've learned what slow travel means and why it offers a more complete experience and is more satisfying than other travel philosophies. You may also have been surprised to discover that, despite all we regularly hear and see in the news, traveling the world is as safe as staying at home.

You have embraced the reasons why it is important for you to travel and to do so while you are still young enough to enjoy it to the fullest. You have identified the amazing places that you would like to visit on your trip and you have discovered how to tie your destinations together into a cohesive adventure. You have also taken into account the timing of the seasons to determine the ideal order for visiting each region on your itinerary and you have considered the various modes of transportation you can use to travel from one region to another.

After learning why slow travel is more economical and more rewarding than a typical vacation, you now know how you can afford to take time away from your career to travel. You also know how to navigate the separation from work and your loved ones and transition to full-time traveling. You have discovered how to organize your current life so you can manage it remotely, as well as how you can stay healthy while traveling. You have also learned what to pack for your adventure and how you can overcome common roadblocks.

While the preparation may seem like a lot of work at times, it can also be an exciting process in itself, and let me assure you that every bit of it is worth it. My wish for you is that someday soon you will be taking in a breathtaking vista or sipping a cappuccino at a sidewalk cafe and looking back fondly at this period of your life. You will be amazed at how far you have come and be both thankful and grateful to your earlier self for taking the leap and going through with it. You will realize with 20/20 vision all that you have gained by stepping boldly forward and following your heart. Because of your inspired actions and persistence, you have successfully brought your dreams to life and now you get to experience them with all of your senses in full technicolor.

If you let them, your travels will provide you an opportunity to experience a significant transformation within yourself. You will start to not only see the world differently than you did before, but you will likely also start to see yourself differently. You will learn to appreciate whole new perspectives that you've never been exposed to before and you may even begin to question many of the prior assumptions you've had about the world and your place in it. These types of growth changes will be happening inside of you a little at a time every step of the way, yet you might not fully realize the impact of your transformation until after you return home.

My wish for you is that you are able to keep an open heart to all that you experience on your travels. This is the key to enjoying the ride and getting the most from your adventures. It is especially important to notice and pay attention whenever you have a negative reaction to something.

The chances are good that there is an opportunity to learn more about yourself from what at first may seem to be a negative experience.

Please remember to reach out to share the joys of your adventure with others so they too can benefit from your discoveries. There will be those that will ask about your travels to be polite while others will sincerely want to know more about your experiences. As you learn to figure out each person's level of interest, you will find that you'll be able to gauge how much information to share in each situation.

I wish for you love, freedom, peace, and wonder as you explore this great planet of ours. The world truly is an amazing place. Now it's time for you to see and experience it for yourself.

Happy Travels!

ACKNOWLEDGMENTS

feel a tremendous amount of gratitude toward everyone who helped to bring this book to life. The journey has been longer than I first realized and there are many people who played their part along the way.

Debbie Slobe, Jamie Seemiller, and many others first planted the seed several years ago at a time when writing a book was possibly the furthest thought from my mind. Melanie Cahill, Lorna Scott, Kathleen Scherek, and Julie Helmrich each in their own way encouraged me to focus on sharing my passion for travel with others. Rex Anderson provided consistent moral support through the ups and downs of figuring it all out. Lisa Adriana Chang has kept me grounded and has taught me how to stay true to my heart. Kit and Randy Cassingham helped me stay true to my message even when I doubted myself.

During a pivotal conversation over dinner and a few beers one night, Shari Czar helped me develop my voice by spontaneously recording my impromptu travel stories on my phone. Her encouragement and unbridled enthusiasm helped me to realize that there are people who would truly benefit from what I have to offer. That conversation opened my eyes and changed my life. Shari, thank you very much for sharing your vision and your perspective with me.

Michael Brownlee provided a crucial bit of advice without really knowing much about me or that I had even been considering writing a book. Yet somehow, he saw in me a deep desire to make a difference and he knew exactly how to help me do that. Michael's suggestion and his insightful advice were exactly what I needed at that particular moment in time. Thank you so much, Michael, for sharing your wisdom with me. If you hadn't done so, this project might never have gotten off the ground.

Michael and the other members of our Mountain Mastermind group gave me excellent clutch advice on how to find the time to write when I already had very full days. To Kristen Carter, David Paul Carter, Lynda Spann, Jay Arthur, Tina Harlow, and Kit Cassingham, thank you very much for offering your best tips for consistently carving out creative time. The results of heeding that advice are now in front of you.

To the Morgan James Publishing team: Special thanks to David Hancock, CEO & Founder for believing in me and my message. To my Author Relations Manager, Bonnie

Rauch, thanks for making the process seamless and easy. Many more thanks to everyone else, but especially Jim Howard, Bethany Marshall, and Nickcole Watkins.

My dear uncle, Tom Jefferson, unhesitatingly provided the resources that I needed to get this project started properly. Thank you from the bottom of my heart for believing in me when I most needed it.

To my sisters, Heather Donahue, Nancy McQuade, and Susan Molineux, and to my parents, Michael and Marianne Myrick: Thank you for always listening to my wild and crazy travel ideas and still loving and supporting me anyway.

I owe so much to my husband, Witt. For over 20 years, you have been my best friend, travel partner, and source of continual loving support. From the time when we first met, you saw the glimmer in my eye when you told me about your travels. You went on to fan those flames by showing me personally how wonderful international travel can be. I love that we get to share all of our life adventures together. Thank you for always being there for me.

I'd also like to give a special shout out to my son, Quinn. You are the light of my life. I am so fortunate to be your mom and it brings me joy to be able to share this great world with you. Thank you for being you.

To paraphrase the immortal words of Bill Patterson from *Calvin and Hobbes*, "It's a magical world, let's go exploring."

THANK YOU

Thank you so much for taking this journey with me. I would be honored if you would also stay in touch to share your success stories and travel adventures. You can reach me via email at Jen@SlowTravelBook.com. I look forward to hearing the details from you about how your life has been transformed in making the bold decision to follow your dreams.

In gratitude and appreciation to you for taking this journey with me, I invite you to visit my website (http://slowtravelbook.com/FreeGift) so you can receive the free travel assessment that I have created just for you. By answering ten simple questions you'll find out how ready you are to slow travel. You will also find a complete list of travel resources there (http://slowtravelbook.com/Resources). I keep that list up-to-date with the latest tips and relevant information to assist you with your travel plans.

ABOUT THE AUTHOR

Jennifer Sparks is a recovering rocket scientist who has always had a passion for travel. While she didn't get her first passport until she was in her late 20s, once she had it, she made sure she got a lot of use out of it. As someone who has never had much affinity for cruises and all-inclusive resorts, she quickly adopted the slow travel philosophy to get more enjoyment out of every travel experience. Through the years, she has traveled by bicycle, car, camper van, backpack, train, bus, tuk-tuk, taxi, bulldozer, ferry, sailboat, and airplane (small and large).

Her biggest travel adventures so far have included traveling in her own car across multiple continents. In 2003, Jen and her husband, Witt, shipped their Land Rover from the US to Southampton, UK. From there, they traveled through 23 countries until they reached Cape Town, South Africa, one year later.

After returning home and settling down for a while, Jen gave birth to their son, Quinn. She was knee-deep in diapers when she realized that she wanted to travel again. So she and Witt started planning their next big adventure to travel through the Americas by camper van. After 19 more countries and two and a half fabulous years on the road, this family of three returned home to the US to allow Quinn to grow some roots. They currently reside in Montrose, Colorado, where they can enjoy mountain life to its fullest while planning their next travel adventure.

Jen's love of travel has been reinforced over and over by the wonderful experiences that she and her family have had. While initially a nervous traveler, she has come to appreciate that, with the right preparation, traveling can be as safe as staying at home. She believes that the path to a more peaceful planet is for many of us to realize just how similar we all are, despite our differences in language and culture. She encourages others to venture forth to experience our amazing planet and its people.

Website: http://SlowTravelBook.com

Email: Jen@SlowTravelBook.com

Facebook: https://www.facebook.com/slowtravel4u/

Instagram: https://www.instagram.com/slow_travel_4u/

9 781642 792287